SH

Born in 1939 in Va̶̶̶̶̶̶̶̶̶̶̶̶̶̶ught up in the West Country, Trevor Housby has travelled the world in his varying capacities as writer, photographer, guitarist, and angler extraordinary. More specifically, he has played a major role in developing new opportunities for shark fishing in British waters, by opening up hitherto untried areas and advocating the use of the sporting light-tackle technique.

A prolific author, an acknowledged master of the art of making his own fishing tales come true, consultant to tourist boards and hordes of frustrated anglers – he is perhaps the most noted angler writing in this country today.

*Pan Anglers' Library*

# SHORE FISHING

(Previously published as *Rock Fishing*)

## TREVOR HOUSBY

**REVISED EDITION**

**PAN BOOKS LTD**
**LONDON AND SYDNEY**

First published 1969 as *Rock Fishing* by Herbert Jenkins Ltd
This revised edition published 1974 by Pan Books Ltd,
Cavaye Place, London SW10 9PG

ISBN 0 330 24124 9

*Printed and bound in England by
Hazell Watson & Viney Ltd,
Aylesbury, Bucks*

TO MY MOTHER

# CONTENTS

# CHAPTER 1

# Shore Fishing

In recent years shore fishing has become an increasingly popular sport. Most anglers in this country live within reasonable travelling distance of good beach, rock, and harbour fishing and in most places a wide variety of fish can be caught. Shore fishing has the added advantage of cheapness; with one or two rare exceptions most sections of shoreline are open to the public and for little more than the cost of tackle, fuel and bait, any British angler can go and catch fish without worrying about day tickets, permits and the like.

Many anglers combine a day's shore fishing with a day out with the family. Others, more dedicated, fish long, hard hours in a serious attempt to catch more and better fish. Either way, shore fishing can be great fun and when the fish are feeding, the catch makes a valuable addition to the family food supply.

Where I live on the south coast of England, local beaches are often lined with anglers. In other less populated areas, anglers are often fortunate enough to have vast sections of coastline to themselves. Round Scotland, for example, there are a great many shore stations which have never been fished; the potential of these out-of-the-way places is fantastic.

Even on overcrowded beaches, good catches can be made, and many anglers in my locality specialize in night fishing to avoid the daytime crowds. Many fish on the British List can be taken from the shore, including certain species of shark. Successful shore anglers spend a great deal of time learning as much as possible about their favourite sections of coastline. Their knowledge of tides, fish movement and marine life helps them catch more and bigger fish and I would advise any angler who takes up shore fishing to choose a particular fishing venue, learn as much as possible about it and stick to it for at least two or three seasons. Constant change of fishing ground seldom produces big fish or big catches.

Shore fishing can be great fun and in most areas there are thriving fishing clubs whose members concentrate on shore fishing. Membership of an existing club of this kind can be a great advantage to both the novice and the experienced angler alike. Most angling clubs hold regular competitions and these, too, can add interest to a normal day's fishing.

## Safety First on Rocks and Beaches

Safety precautions should be a matter of common sense, but far too many shore fishermen fail to observe the signs and far too many accidents or near-accidents occur each season. All anglers make a mistake now and again, and become so engrossed with their fishing that they fail to notice that the rising tide has crept round behind them, filled up a gully which an hour before was dry and which now cuts them off completely from the mainland. When this sort of thing occurs the angler is obliged to wade or swim across the gully, getting thoroughly wet in the process, or to stay put until the tide goes out again – if, of course, the rock upon which he is standing doesn't get covered over by the rising tide. Even if it doesn't, a rising wind and a big breaker can soon lift a man off a rock and drown him. Personally, I would rather get wet in the first place by crossing the water-filled gully.

Again, don't fail to take notice of the high tide mark. This is easy to define by the line of dried weed, roots, driftwood and other rubbish left behind by the sea. More important still is to move steadily back as the tide rises, so that by the time full tide is reached, you will be fishing from a safe place. Don't climb down cliffs unless you are absolutely certain that you can get back up them easily, and never drop down sheer walls of rock to reach a likely vantage point, for if a hand- or foothold is six inches out of reach when you come to make the return journey, those few inches may be enough to drown you. Crêpe- or leather-soled shoes, studded boots and similar footwear should be avoided if you intend to rock fish. Weedy rocks are treacherous at any time, and when wearing shoes of these types, they can be ankle-breakers. Good wellington, or thigh boots with cleated rubber soles are suitable for scrambling over slippery rock; even these are not ideal, but providing one pays careful attention to each foothold they will give good service.

Generally it is best to rock fish in company, for then, if an accident does occur, help is near at hand. Far pastures, of course, always look greener and anglers are always keen to break away from the normal venues to try other likely-looking spots. Along the south coast of Cornwall this urge to explore and fish unknown rock marks leads to a number of accidents, usually of the cliff fall type for, although solid enough at first glance, many Cornish cliffs are rotten, and a rock which appeared to be able to stand the weight of an elephant will suddenly shatter when used as a hand- or foothold. This can be extremely dangerous for an angler will be carrying his rods and tackle in one hand and will be placing all his faith on the other. Consequently, if the rock suddenly disintegrates he will probably fall. Even a short fall on to sharp rock can be very nasty and a long fall can be fatal. Worse still is the fact that other people will have to risk their own lives in a rescue bid. Believe me, local coastguards and fishermen have more than enough to do without spending their time worrying about you, so think twice before taking foolish chances; and if it is a matter of losing your life or your tackle, then get rid of the tackle. You can always buy more but can't buy a new life. This then is a picture of the hazardous side of rock fishing. Approached sensibly, none of the accidents described should happen. Think before you act and then move cautiously. By doing this you will have no trouble and gain many happy hours of good fishing.

# CHAPTER 2

# Bass

Along the south and south-west coasts of England, Wales and Ireland, bass are a favourite quarry of many shore fishermen. Tide-washed headlands are ideal places to fish, for bass of all sizes delight in rough water and fast tide races, and they find a great deal of food in such places. Bass are basically predatory fish which live mainly on small fish. Prawns, and sand eels, marine worms and shellfish are also eaten in large quantities. Very big bass are great scavengers and will happily pick up and eat any edible rubbish they come across. Small bass, on the other hand, are rather clean feeders, and spend most of their time in pursuit of live fresh food. After reaching a weight of five to seven pounds, however, the fish usually change and become true scavengers, although they are still happy to eat any small live fish they find. It is difficult to decide at what weight a bass becomes a true specimen, for the average run of fish fluctuates considerably from one area to another. As a rough guide it is safe to regard a 7 lb to 8 lb fish as a good catch and anything over 10 lb as a true specimen. Bass above 13 lb in weight are extremely rare, although the bass record stands at over 18 lb. Very small bass are usually called 'checkers', while fish between one and two pounds are referred to as 'schoolies' or school bass.

There is a tendency for anglers to kill all the bass they catch, irrespective of size. This is a short-sighted policy, for by returning the smaller fish alive and unharmed, sport in future years can be ensured. Indiscriminate slaughter can have a bad and long-lasting effect, and in some areas where bass were once commonly caught, these fish are now only taken on rare occasions, proof indeed that conservation is essential. Even where big bass are concerned, the intelligent angler should set himself a bag limit, and return all fish over and above this limit which he catches. There is little point in killing a lot of big fish which can't be used.

There can be little doubt that bass fishing is good sport; bass of all sizes are fast-moving, game fighters, which can provide great sport on lightish tackle. From this angle, the shore angler is fortunate for as most shore-caught bass are taken at close range, it is seldom necessary to use the heavy beach casting outfits which are essential for beach fishing for other fish. It is amazing just how close to the shore the bass swim, and most successful shore anglers dispense altogether with long casting techniques where bass are concerned, and concentrate on fishing as close as possible to the beach. They are extremely shy and are quick to take fright at the first sign of danger. Because of this, the shore angler will be well advised to wear dark clothes, and to refrain from moving about too much while bass fishing. Under no circumstances should the angler stand silhouetted against the skyline. Always sit or crouch when fishing from exposed rocks, otherwise sport will be very poor indeed.

Although bass are basically summer visitors, they can still be caught during the late autumn and winter months on many coasts. These late season bass are usually of a larger average size than the summer-caught fish, although rather few and far between. This is the time of the year when really big bass come inshore, and any sea angler who has easy access to a good bass fishing area will be well advised to fish hard during September, October and early November.

## Optimum Fishing Times

Although plenty of good bass are taken by daytime anglers, the best time to go bass fishing is at night. Dawn has long been considered a good time to catch them, but it seems likely that the bass that are taken at this time are just at the end of a night-feeding session, and many modern bass specialists now make a point of fishing right through the night. There can be little doubt that bass of all sizes move right inshore as darkness

13

falls. There have been many outstanding catches taken by night anglers fishing areas which normally produce very poor results to the daytime fishermen. Obviously a rising tide which coincides with darkness is ideal for bass fishing, but I have known of several very big bass which have been taken at night when the tide has been dead low.

## Tackle

For float fishing, spinning and general light fishing methods a rod and reel of the type described in the wrasse chapter is ideal, but for bottom fishing with heavy tackle and large baits something more substantial will be required. When choosing a set of tackle for this kind of angling, it is wise to bear in mind the type of ground that will mainly be fished and also the strength of tide which will be encountered. Having calculated this, it is simple enough to choose a set of well-balanced tackle which will be a pleasure to use. If, for example, you intend to fish mainly from weed-fringed rocks which jut directly out into a sandy bay where strongish tides prevail, a 12 ft or 13 ft rod capable of casting 4 to 6 oz weights will be essential, for the length of the rod will enable hooked fish to be kept away from the seaweed fringe round the rocks, which would be practically impossible if a shorter rod were used, and at the same time, the long rod will keep the line between rod tip and weight above this weed so that the line cannot tangle during the time spent waiting for a bite. A long rod also has the strength to throw a heavy weight accurately. For fishing in rock gullies where long casting is unnecessary, a shorter rod capable of handling weights up to 3 oz is more useful, for as the bait will be presented almost under the rod tip, it will be simple to set a hook and control a running fish with a shorter rod. Choice of reel for bottom fishing is a matter of personal preference, though a good quality multiplier is recommended, as these are more robust than even a large fixed-spool reel, and once properly mastered are easy to use.

Bass of all sizes are predatory, and it is common to catch tiny school bass on artificial lures almost as large as themselves. Bass will take worm, crab and shellfish baits as well as fish. In areas where sand eels are common, huge shoals of bass gather to harry these bright little fish. Consequently live or dead sand eels make first-class bass baits. Elvers can also be used and in Cornwall I have had many good bass on these slippery little

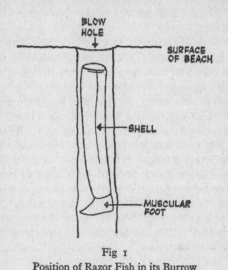

Fig 1
Position of Razor Fish in its Burrow

baits. When casting from rocks which are flanked by sandy ground razor fish can be used to deadly effect. These shellfish (fig 1) live in sand where they spend their entire lives in a vertical position. When disturbed they dig rapidly into the sand to a depth of several feet. They do this by means of a long muscular fleshy foot. Razor fish are rather difficult to locate, but they give their positions away by ejecting a stream of water from their shells as they begin to dig downwards. Once located they can either be dug out of their holes or they can be induced to rise to the surface simply by pouring a quantity of plain salt down their tunnels. This is more effective when followed by a quantity of water. This salt and water treatment causes the razor fish to shoot to the surface of the beach, where it stops with about half an inch of shell protruding above the sand. Once it does this it can easily be extracted from its hole. Razor fish can also be gathered by means of a wire spear which is pushed down the blow hole until the fish is felt, then twisted so that the end of the wire spear catches in the firm flesh of the razor fish. Once this happens, a strong steady pull will bring it to the surface.

Expert bass fishermen say that soft or peeler crab make the best bait of all for bass. This is a rather sweeping statement, but I must say that crab baits catch more than a fair share of fish and large bass in particular respond extremely well to crab baits. Shore crabs change their shells at least once a year, and during the first stage of this act the old shell splits down the middle. In this state the crab is known as a 'peeler': later, when the old shell has dropped cleanly away and the crab is busy growing a new one, it is known as a 'softie'. During both these stages the crabs are much sought after as bait, and in many areas anglers construct little traps out of stones and old tiles which the moulting crabs use in the mistaken belief they have found a safe refuge from the many dangers which constantly threaten them. Under normal circumstances, loose

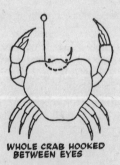

**WHOLE CRAB HOOKED
BETWEEN EYES**

Fig 2

weed-covered rocks are the places to search, for these provide soft and peeler crabs with a natural refuge.

Soft crabs should be used whole, and the hook should be passed either through the back of the crab or through the soft shell between the eyes (fig 2). Peeler crabs should be stripped of their shell and used either whole or, in the case of big crabs, in halves. Peeler crabs are soft and it pays to tie the bait to the hook with a short length of darning wool or elastic thread (fig 3). Bass are active hunters, and when hungry will also eat hard-backed crabs. In fact, most of the bass that are caught contain at least one hard-backed crab and often a lot more than one. Yet few anglers ever try bass fishing with a hard-backed crab as bait.

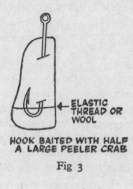

← ELASTIC THREAD OR WOOL

HOOK BAITED WITH HALF A LARGE PEELER CRAB

Fig 3

## METHODS

### Spinning for Bass

For the energetic angler who likes to cover a good deal of ground, one of the nicest and most effective methods to employ is spinning, for armed only with a light rod, reel and a haversack to hold spare tackle, a flask and some food, the spin fisherman can make his way easily from one likely spot to the next, covering a large area of water en route. Bass of all sizes respond well to artificial baits, and on many days when the bottom fishermen find it hard to catch fish, the spinning rod will account for good bags of prime bass. Artificial baits are legion and it is easy to overspend when purchasing new lures. Many anglers become avid collectors of lures, and habitually carry a vast selection of brightly coloured baits which they seldom use. To avoid becoming a collector, it is advisable to limit one's choice of lures so that only a practical selection is carried. Spinning round weed-covered rocks is at best a costly business and even the most experienced anglers must be prepared to lose

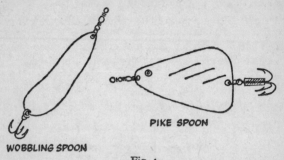

PIKE SPOON

WOBBLING SPOON

Fig 4

quite a few baits during the course of an average day. Because of this only the less expensive lures should be employed.

There are many suitable lures available, and where bass are concerned the larger and flashier the bait is, the better it seems to work. Long Swedish wobbling spoons and plain pike spoons

COLORADO
SPOON

Fig 5

(fig 4) are firm favourites with knowledgeable bass anglers. Colorado spoons (fig 5) are also effective. These are fitted with red woollen tails which should be removed before use, for the wool will hold salt water which in turn will quickly corrode the hooks. Single and jointed plugs (fig 6) make good baits, but are expensive and have a tendency to snag up. Blue and white-coloured plugs seem to make the best baits. A bait which is extremely good for bass fishing is the old-fashioned wagtail lure (fig 7). These are normally coloured red and gold or blue

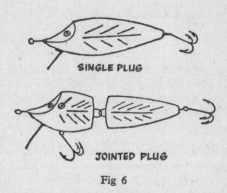

SINGLE PLUG

JOINTED PLUG

Fig 6

and silver. Like the plug baits already mentioned, blue seems to be the most killing colour. Wagtails have the advantage of being soft baits, which makes them more attractive to a taking fish than metal, wood or plastic lures. There are a wide range of plastic prawns, crabs, squid, etc on the market but these are designed to catch anglers more than fish and are best left alone.

WAGTAIL

Fig 7

For short-range work it is seldom necessary to add any form of lead weight to the terminal tackle; with light tackle the weight of the bait will be sufficient for casting purposes. When extra-long casting is called for, a supplementary weight can be added, the cheapest and simplest being a plain barrel lead stopped at either end by a large soft split shot (fig 8). This

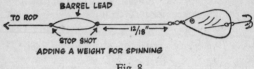

Fig 8

should be positioned 12 in to 18 in from the bait. Although bass obviously hunt close to the sea bed, they seem to take an artificial bait best when it is worked at mid-water. To do this properly, the bait should be retrieved at a steady, even pace. To vary the movement of the lure, the rod tip can be swung steadily from side to side so that the lure doesn't follow too

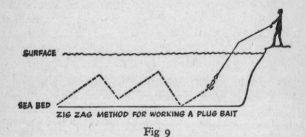

Fig 9

straight a line. Plugs should be worked in jerks so that they follow a zig-zag up and down path (fig 9).

Hungry bass usually take a bait in a savage fashion, often hooking themselves in the process. These are occasions, however, when the fish will continually follow the bait without attempting to attack it. This sort of behaviour can be most frustrating, for it usually occurs on bright windless days when the sea is calm and clear enough for the following bass to be clearly seen. The only way I have ever found to tempt the fish when they are in this finicky mood is to change to a very tiny bright bait. This will often do the trick, although many fish may be lost on the strike due to the small hooks failing to engage. As a general rule large lures are best, for bass are voracious fish which have big mouths and appetites to match. Bass love rough waters and it pays to spin the most disturbed areas as thoroughly as possible, for they are ever on the lookout for food in such places and will take a spinner well under these conditions.

*Float Fishing*

One of the pleasantest and most rewarding ways of taking bass is to float fish from rocks and jetties which are surrounded by fairly deep water. Bass find a great deal of natural food in these places and by presenting a natural bait on float tackle close to the rock face, good catches can often be made. One of the commonest faults of the modern angler is the constant desire to cast farther than his neighbour. The blame for this can be laid squarely on the fixed-spool reel which is so simple to use that even the complete novice can throw a long line without any preliminary practice. The ability to cast farther than everyone else doesn't always lead to large catches, and where bass are concerned it is often advisable to just swing the tackle out a few yards: otherwise it is easy to overshoot the most likely feeding areas.

Live prawns are one of the deadliest bass baits, and an hour spent using a baited drop net in a sheltered weedy rock gully will usually produce enough prawns for a complete day's fishing. Prawns are very delicate and should be handled carefully and gently. For transportation, they should be placed in a large container filled with clear sea water. This water should be changed at frequent intervals to ensure that the prawns remain active and lively. Although dead prawns will still attract fish, they work best when used alive. Because of this, great care should be taken to mount the prawn properly on the hook (fig 10).

HOW TO HOOK A LIVE PRAWN

Fig 10

Bulky floats are not much good for bass fishing, particularly when light baits are used. One of the finest bass floats I have ever used was given to me by Major D. F. Kelley who is well known for his writings on both bass and wrasse fishing. Major Kelley calls this float a balsa pencil (fig 11) for it is shaped like

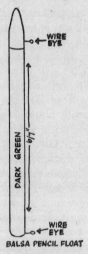

WIRE EYE

DARK GREEN

6″

WIRE EYE

BALSA PENCIL FLOAT

Fig 11

an oval carpenter's pencil. The one I use is approximately 6 in long, and for its size and shape it is able to support a remarkable amount of lead. At the same time it is extremely sensitive and is one of the finest sea floats I have ever used. Except under special circumstances fixed floats are seldom of much use to the sea angler, and the balsa pencil is made up with wire rings so that it slides freely on the line. Bass feed at all depths but it is best to set the float so that the bait is suspended at or around the mid-water mark. This is particularly important when prawns or worms are used as bait, for if these are presented too close to the bottom the ever-present wrasse will find them long before the bass come on the scene. Fish strip baits (fig 12) can also be used on float tackle, but these are standby baits which seldom produce results like the more natural baits.

FISH STRIP BAIT

Fig 12

In the West Country where sand eels are common, many bass anglers use these delicate little fish to the exclusion of all other baits, and some magnificent catches of large bass have been taken on the natural eel. Unfortunately, sand eels die very quickly when confined in a bait can, but even a dead sand eel makes quite good bait provided it is fresh. The best way of collecting a supply of sand eels is to use a special two-pronged fork (fig 13). This is used to rake eels out of the damp sand at the water's edge. There is a knack to this, but once the technique is mastered, it is a simple operation to collect a plentiful

SAND EEL FORK

Fig 13

supply of bait-sized sand eels. There are several ways of attaching a live sand eel to a hook, the best being to pass the hook point and barb through the lower jaw of the eel (fig 14). Another effective method is to pass the hook through the flesh directly behind the head of the bait (fig 14). A disadvantage of

LIP HOOKED SAND EEL

BACK HOOKED SAND EEL

Fig 14

this method is that baits hooked in this way die rather quickly. Sand eels are fragile fish and seldom stand up to the shock of being cast any distance. The correct way of casting sand eel-baited float tackle is to swing it out gently so that the bait drops as softly as possible into the water.

Bass usually bite boldly on float tackle and consequently are fairly easy to hook. Largish hooks are, however, an advantage and a size 2 or 1 freshwater-scale hook is ideal.

## True Livebaiting

Bass are fast-moving active hunters and in rocky areas they eat large numbers of small fish, immature wrasse, pouting, rockling, etc, being the main quarry of the hungry bass. Because of this, livebaiting can be a most useful method, although few anglers seem to realize the potential of the technique. The easiest way of presenting a small livebait is on float tackle, for unless the bait is supported well above the sea bed it will quickly take refuge among the rocks or weeds and snag the tackle. A livebait is far heavier than a prawn or sand eel, and to support the extra weight a more substantial float is necessary. The float I find most useful is a large-diameter pike pilot float. These can be improved by inserting a short length of plastic tube through the bored centre hole in the float (fig 15). This

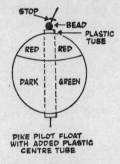

Fig 15

will stop the reel line from cutting into the actual cork body of the float when the strike is made. A float of this type slides freely, supports a large bait, and offers little resistance to a taking fish. Pouting make first-class bass baits, but small wrasse and rock fish collected from tide pools at low water are almost as good.

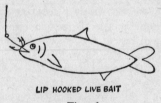

LIP HOOKED LIVE BAIT

Fig 16

When livebaiting a single size 4 or 6 treble hook gives more hooking power than a larger single hook and for this reason is preferable (fig 16). Once a bass takes a livebait it must be given enough time to get the bait well into its mouth. A premature strike will only pull the livebait away from the fish; the correct procedure is to give the taking fish line until enough time has elapsed for the fish to have turned the bait and started to swallow it. As a rough guide, count slowly up to ten before striking. This will usually give the fish sufficient time to get the bait well inside its jaws. One successful bass angler I know always hooks livebaits through the root of the tail (fig 17).

LIVEBAIT TAIL HOOKED

Fig 17

Frankly, I can see no advantage in this method, except on days when the bass are in a playful mood and are content to just nip at the bait's tail instead of taking it properly.

## Bottom Fishing

Bass of all sizes will browse over the sea bed in search of food and bottom fishing can be a most productive pastime. The only time bottom fishing from rocks is practical is when the rocks are surrounded by a clean sand or gravel bottom. Clean-bottomed gullies are also likely places, but for true bottom fishing it is advisable to select a rocky outcrop which projects into a sandy bay or beach. A one- or two-hook running leger (fig 18) is suitable for this type of fishing, although a single-

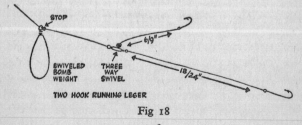

STOP

6/9"

SWIVELED BOMB WEIGHT

THREE WAY SWIVEL

18/24"

TWO HOOK RUNNING LEGER

Fig 18

boom paternoster (fig 19) can also be used. Whenever possible, an extra long trace should be used, for a bait which moves about over a fairly wide area will be far more attractive to the bass than a bait which is presented on a short trace. Bottom fishing tackle often accounts for those extra large bass which so many shore anglers dream about.

My own experiences with bottom fishing have led me to believe that the 'big baits for big fish' idea certainly works where bass are concerned. There are of course exceptions to any rule, but generally a large bait produces fish of a higher than normal average size. Whole fish, squid heads and kipper fillets all work very well, kipper fillet being extremely good, for despite the

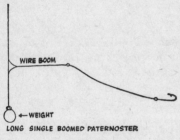

LONG SINGLE BOOMED PATERNOSTER

Fig 19

fact that it has been cured, kipper still contains a great deal of oil and as bass seem to like a smelly bait the kipper often produces bites when fresh baits fail. Squid heads or small squid used whole (fig 20) are first-class baits, so too are small dead rock fish.

These baits may seem large to anglers who are used to bass fishing with worm baits, but bass have big mouths and appetites to match and as specialist freshwater anglers have proved, by thinking big you catch big fish. This applies to all species, but bass in particular lend themselves to this idea. Years ago while bottom fishing for conger in a series of deep rock gullies situated near my Cornish home I found I was getting a number of fast bites on my large mackerel fillet baits. The sheer speed with which the bait was taken told me that it wasn't conger that were responsible and for some time these strange bites puzzled me. Then one day I managed to make contact with one of the mystery fish and found to my surprise that it was a bass and a good one at that. This first fish weighed nearly 9 lb and other fish I caught on later outings were of a similar large size. Why a normally cautious fish like the bass should deign to take a big fish fillet mounted on a large hook attached to a thick wire trace is beyond me and I can only assume that big bass are greedy creatures and are quite content to make a grab at a large bait. Since this period, I have concentrated on big baits while bot-

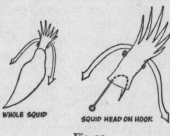

WHOLE SQUID        SQUID HEAD ON HOOK

Fig 20

tom fishing for bass, and my results have proved to me that this has been a good idea, for I have caught a number of fine bass which I am sure would never have turned their heads for a single worm bait.

Bass fishing is exciting and fascinating and many anglers specialize in this one species. The shore angler can easily specialize in this way, for bass of all sizes visit shore marks regularly and offer fine sport to the angler who is prepared to work hard for his fish.

When fishing small coves and bays it is advisable to take careful notice of any natural features which are likely to attract bass. A small inflowing stream of fresh water often interests bass, for the fresh water attracts elvers and sand eels, upon both of which bass feed. A single rock projecting above the sand is another good bass-holding spot and a bait cast out to fall close to an outcrop of this kind will usually catch more fish than a bait which is cast out into a flat barren stretch of sand. The reason that bass hang round small projecting rocks is obvious, for the action of the tide on the rock dislodges all sorts of edible creatures which the waiting bass are quick to snap up. Peeler crabs or sand eels are as good a bait as any to use under those conditions, for both are natural, and both are likely to be found sheltering under or close to the rock. Bass are often bold biters and some anglers are content to jam their rods into a suitable crevice or into a rod-stand and sit back to wait for a bass to hook itself. This is lazy angling and not to be recommended, for many good bites will be missed completely. Personally, I don't like to use a rod-rest of any description while bass fishing; I find that by holding my rod at all times I catch far more bass than the lazy angler, and miss very few reasonable bites on the strike. My usual technique is to hold the rod so that the line between rod tip and bait is taut and at the first suggestion of a bite I drop the rod tip slightly so that the fish is free to take a little line, then I strike at the next definite indication of a bite. Far too many anglers make a hash of striking, probably by becoming over-excited. Self-discipline is essential and should be learnt at an early stage. Once you have learned to control your initial reactions, striking can become an automatic reflex action, but control must be learned. Far too many anglers snatch wildly at the rod at the first sign of a bite. This habit will catch few fish, particularly bass which are generally cautious feeders.

# CHAPTER 3

# Cod Fishing

Shore fishing for cod is never as productive as boat fishing, but the fact remains that a cod which tipped the scales at 44 lb was caught by a young Welsh angler while fishing a rock mark near his home. Cod of this calibre are rarely encountered by commercial fishermen let alone rod-and-line enthusiasts and, as a general rule, a thirty-pounder caught from a boat can justifiably be regarded as a really fine achievement. Whether or not a fish over this weight will ever be caught from the shore remains to be seen, but my guess is that it will be a good many years before this great fish is beaten. In most areas cod are rightly regarded as a winter species, the only exception being found in Scotland's prolific waters where cod and codling can be caught at most times of the year by shore anglers.

Cod are generally a fish of the northern seas, but can be found in small numbers all round our coasts. In the winter the south coast of England is visited by vast shoals of big cod, which have proved first-class sport for the boat and shore angler alike. Probably the most famous south coast 'hot spot' for cod is Dungeness beach in Kent, but of recent years the cod shoals have started to move even farther south than this, and good catches of shore-caught cod are now taken regularly as far down as Chesil beach. So far, there has been no scientific explanation as to why the cod shoals are moving farther south each winter, but the effect of this movement is being felt as far down as South Cornwall where cod, which were once regarded as rare visitors, are now being caught in increasing numbers by boat fishermen. It is interesting to note also that the average size of cod caught from these 'new' cod fishing areas is extremely high, most fish being between 16 lb and 25 lb. Why the smaller fish aren't being caught no one can say; so far, the smaller fish just don't seem to have wandered down from the Kent and Sussex marks. A big cod is an ugly fish which under no circumstances could be described as graceful. It has a big head, pot belly and is far too narrow at the tail to have an attractive outward appearance. The snout of the cod protrudes beyond its mouth and the upper jaw is longer than its lower jaw. The jaws are well armed with sharp little teeth and its lips are thick and fleshy. There is a conspicuous barbel under its chin, and its small scales give it a smooth feel when handled. Cod vary considerably in colour from one location to another. Generally, big cod are greyish green and are spotted along the back and sides with golden- or greenish-brown blotches. The belly of the fish is invariably white. Cod caught over rocky ground have a tendency to be rather redder than those caught over sand or gravel. In Scotland the fish I caught from rock marks were a lovely reddish-brown colour. These particular fish were caught among thick beds of kelp which were growing on solid rock. The light-coloured lateral line is very pronounced.

Cod are voracious fish and will eat practically any edible object that comes their way. Crustaceans, molluscs, echinoderms (generally starfish) and small fish are consumed in large numbers. Herrings and sprats are a favourite food of big cod, but pouting, whiting, dragonets and small flatfish are also eaten when available. Cod are prolific fish, and a ripe 20 lb to 30 lb female is estimated to shed well over six million eggs at a time. Naturally, the mortality rate among both the eggs and the fry of the cod is high. This is no doubt a good thing, for if the majority of cod eggs hatched and matured, there would be no other fish in our seas. Cod grow fairly rapidly and a six-year-old fish should weigh around 15 lb. The largest cod on record weighed 211½ lb. This monster was caught in American waters. British trawlers working Arctic grounds occasionally catch fish up to 80 lb in weight. Fish of this calibre are unlikely to fall to the rod-and-line angler, but the average size of inshore cod is generally large enough to satisfy the big fish enthusiast.

Cod are rarely encountered on their own and where one is caught there should be others. I have no doubt that when enough shore fishermen explore the winter fishing potential of Scottish waters, some remarkable cod catches will be made. As yet, very little summer fishing let alone winter fishing is done around the Scottish coasts but it won't be very long now before southern anglers start to visit these waters in ever-increasing numbers.

## Feeding Habits

To catch big cod in inshore waters the shore angler must be prepared to fish at night, for although boat anglers consistently bring large cod to the gaff during the daytime it is rare for these big fish to venture into shallow water until nightfall. There are, of course, exceptions to this rule but generally speaking daytime angling will only yield catches of codling. Codling average 3 lb to 6 lb in weight and often bite freely during the daytime. The big fish, however, are more cautious than their smaller brethren. Cod of all sizes will eat anything edible that they can find, but certain baits are favoured in certain areas and it is rare to find two cod anglers who can agree with each other on the subject of baits. I have found that I can catch cod on a wide variety of baits, no matter where I choose to fish. Consequently I don't worry when I have to use a bait which local experts won't look at.

## Cod Baits

Probably the most popular and most widely used bait is lugworm; ragworms are also good but are more difficult to dig or purchase, and also they tend to break up during casting. This doesn't occur so much when lugworms are used. Lugworms can often be dug in quantity from beaches which are comprised of sand and mud. These worms live in a U-shaped tunnel (fig 21). They move slowly up one arm of this tunnel to breathe and feed, then back up the other arm to deposit the waste matter from their bodies. This waste appears on the surface of the

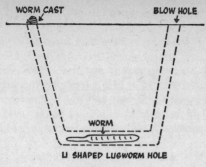

LI SHAPED LUGWORM HOLE

Fig 21

beach as a neat coil of sand. This coil is known as a 'cast' and a careful inspection of the surface surrounding this cast will soon reveal the 'blow hole' of the worm which appears as a small indentation in the sand. The only practical way of collecting worms is to dig for them. There are several methods of doing this. Either you can dig a trench right across the worm beds with a garden fork, or you can dig between the worm 'cast' and the blow hole (fig 22). Lugworm can be used whole, or the tail section can be removed so that the inside of the worm can be squeezed out. Many cod anglers prefer to do this, for the hollow body tube of the worm makes a good tough bait which

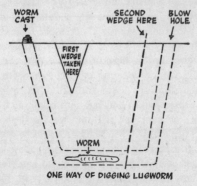

ONE WAY OF DIGGING LUGWORM

Fig 22

33

can be cast a considerable distance without fear of it breaking up. Lugworm can be used singly or in bunches. Cod like big baits and a bunch of up to six worms makes a large and attractive bait.

Fish baits are not generally favoured by cod fishermen but a whole small pouting, or half a fresh herring makes a good bait. Squid makes good bait and my best shore-caught cod which weighed just over 23 lb fell to a whole squid head complete with tentacles. Squid can also be cut up into long strips. These are best used in bunches of three or four (fig 23) so that they wave about with the movement of the water. Cod seem to be greatly attracted by movement and I find bunched squid strip baits to be good fish catchers. Crab, limpet and mussels are also

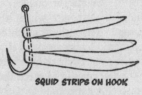

SQUID STRIPS ON HOOK

Fig 23

good. Mussel is a favourite bait among Yorkshire shore anglers. Once again, three or more mussels should be bunched on a single hook. When long casting is necessary to reach the feeding areas, soft wool should be used to tie the mussels on to the hook. To toughen up the flesh of the mussel a good supply of these shellfish should be opened and left exposed to the air for several hours before use. A quicker method is to drop the live mussels into a saucepan of hot, but not boiling water. This will cause the shells to open, and will toughen the flesh at the same time. Cockles are another good cod bait. These are often used by commercial fishermen who catch cod on long lines. I have also used frozen sand eel for cod fishing and have found it to be quite good. Only the largest eels should be used, for small eels are less likely to catch the eye of the foraging cod shoals.

34

Although the cod can never be classed as a real fighting fish, its sheer bulk makes it a tricky proposition to land, and shore fishing for cod is generally regarded as a rugged sport which calls for heavy strong tackle. Ideas differ from one locality to the next and a northern cod specialist uses entirely different tackle to his southern counterpart. There are signs, however, that the newcomers to northern shore fishing are gradually forsaking the traditional northern tackle in favour of the type of outfit used by southern anglers. This is probably due to the new long casting methods devised by southern fishermen, methods which cannot be employed unless the right rods, reels, lines, etc, are used.

## Rods and Reels (Southern Style)

In the south of England most shore-based cod anglers use 11 ft or 12 ft hollow glass beach-casting rods. There are now many patterns available, the best being those incorporating a reverse taper butt (fig 24). This type of rod was devised specifically for beach casting with cod in mind, and for long casting a rod of

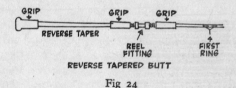

Fig 24

this type cannot be bettered. Unfortunately, a well-finished rod constructed along these lines is an expensive item, and a good one will cost over twenty pounds. This may seem an exorbitant price to pay, but the old adage of 'the best being the cheapest in the long run' should be remembered, and a top quality beach-casting rod will last for years, and will be a constant pleasure to use. These rods are capable of casting a bait a hundred to a hundred and fifty yards depending on the skill and experience of the angler. Long casting certainly pays where cod are concerned and the man who can drop his bait well beyond average casting range will usually catch the most fish.

Beach-casting rods constructed on the reverse tapered butt principle are designed to be used in conjunction with a wide-drum multiplying reel. Once again there are many types available. I personally use a Pflueger Sea King, but the British-made Intrepid Sea Streak, or the American Penn Squidder are just as good. These reels cost between ten and fifteen pounds. The American patterns can be purchased with either metal or plastic spools. Most of the long-casting experts prefer the plastic spools, for being lighter than metal they revolve more easily than the metal spools. The only disadvantage with a plastic spool is that it has a tendency to crack and split when under pressure. This is rather unfortunate, for nylon line contracts when under strain, and this contraction often splits or distorts a reel spool. Because of this, a spare spool should always be carried so that should a breakage of this kind occur during a fishing trip a new spool can be quickly substituted for the broken one. This is one of the prices that has to be paid to gain a few more yards during casting.

Deep narrow-drummed reels should be avoided for these are not designed for long casting and are generally used for boat fishing. Nylon is the best kind of line to use with the rod and reel described. The breaking strain of this line is dependent upon the kind of fishing one expects to do. Beach anglers for example catch many big cod on 20 lb or 23 lb bs lines, but it must be remembered that the beach fisherman is fishing in a comparatively snag-free area, whereas the rock angler will either be casting directly into a jumble of rock and thick weed, or casting over such ground so that his bait drops on sand or gravel. In both cases hooked fish will have to be brought over the rocks and weed before they can be landed. So for this kind of fishing I would recommend the use of a line with a bs of no less than 28 lb. Obviously, the thicker the line diameter the less easy it is to cast but it is better to sacrifice ten or twenty yards on a cast and land most of the fish you hook rather than to gain those extra few yards and get smashed up by every decent cod that comes along.

Cod have long been the favourite quarry of the northern angler,
and the Yorkshire coast is probably the most fished cod area.
Over the years specialized tackle was developed for catching
the cod that lurk off the flat rocks and scaurs of the Yorkshire
coast, and even now this tackle is still in general use and seems
likely to remain popular for some time to come. Ten-foot
double-built cane or plain Burma pole rods are the favourite
weapons of the Yorkshire specialist. These thick powerful rods
are clumsy by southern standards, but for use over rough
ground they are the equal of a hollow glass beach-caster for
they have one great advantage over the soft-actioned glass rods,
which are far too flexible to pull a lead out of rough ground at
the first indication of a bite. The stiff-actioned northern rod
doesn't bend nearly as much as the glass rod which means it
will lift the lead the moment the strike is made. This is a useful
feature for any delay is often fatal; a hooked cod will quickly
shake the hook free unless the rod is powerful enough to lift
the weight and set the hook at the same instant.

By southern standards northern tackle is far too cumbersome, and the huge 7 in Scarborough type reel is no exception. These big narrow-drummed reels are designed for use
with lines of 35 lb to 60 lb bs, far heavier than anything the
southern angler will use for codding but quite normal by Yorkshire standards. In expert hands the stiff rods and Scarborough
type reels can be made to do wonders, and many a northern
angler can cast one hundred yards or more with this kind of
gear. The large-diameter reels are of course ideal for bringing
in fish quickly. This can be an advantage when fishing over
rough ground and shallow water. Casting with tackle of this
kind requires considerable practice, and I am rather afraid that
it is a skill which is without doubt disappearing as more and
more young anglers turn to more modern tackle. In the old
days Scarborough reels were invariably loaded with cuttyhunk
line. For many years now nylon has been used in preference to
this, and it is rare to see a Scarborough tackle specialist employing even a modern braided Terylene or Dacron type line.

Readers will notice that I have made no mention of fixed-spool reels in this chapter, the reason being that I don't consider a fixed spool to be robust enough to stand up to the strain of constant cod fishing without the bale arm becoming broken and distorted. The only other reels which could be used for codding are the Alvey side-cast reels. These are manufactured in Australia and are designed to swivel round (fig 25) so that the reel casts like a fixed-spool reel and retrieves like a centre

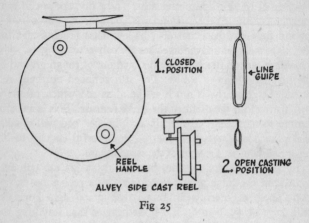

ALVEY SIDE CAST REEL

Fig 25

pin. I have never fished consistently with one of these reels, but understand that they are inclined to twist and kink the line unless a trace incorporating at least two swivels is used.

*Leads*

For casting over rock so that the bait is fished on sand or gravel a plain bomb or pyramid lead is ideal (fig 26). Both are designed for long casting and are weighted at the forward end. Plain leads of this kind are best used in a moderate swell; for rough water a spiked pyramid lead is best (fig 26). The four wire spikes are arranged so that in use at least two of the wires dig into the sand and anchor the lead and bait to the

sea bed. In rough water this is essential, otherwise the lead
and bait will roll with the movement of the water, and eventually the terminal tackle will be swept inshore in a tangled state.
This occasionally occurs even with an anchor weight, but only
in extreme conditions will a lead of the spiked type shift once
it has dug into the sand. For obvious reasons, anchor weights

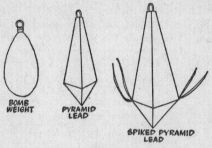

BOMB
WEIGHT

PYRAMID
LEAD

SPIKED PYRAMID
LEAD

Fig 26

should not be used on a rough bottom, otherwise a hang-up
will be inevitable, and even though the anchor wires will·bend
out under pressure, very few really snagged leads will be re-
covered. When fishing right among rocks and weed a flat lead

TWISTED
WIRE ⟶

YORKSHIRE STYLE FLAT LEAD

Fig 27

(fig 27) is best. These weights seldom snag up as much as the
more conventional casting weights already described, and tend
to kite up over the rocks while being retrieved. This type of
weight is sometimes called a Filey or Holderness lead and was
originally designed for codding on the Yorkshire coast. For

39

general cod fishing a 6 oz lead should be employed but in rough seas an 8 oz weight is best.

## Hooks

Even small cod have got large mouths and a range of hooks between 1/0 and 5/0 should always be carried. 3/0 or 4/0 are the most commonly used sizes. There are many patterns available, but for strength and shape the straight-eyed flat forged bronze hooks manufactured by Mustad are about the best

FLAT FORGED MUSTAD HOOK

Fig 28

type to use (fig 28). Beaked barbed-shanked hooks are good, but I find that the long curved point tends to tear out of the cod's mouth; also the long point quickly becomes blunted by contact with stones, shingle, etc. Sharp hooks are essential and a carborundum stone should be a standard part of any angler's equipment, for a few touches with it will soon restore a hook point.

## Methods

For fishing over a flat sand or gravel bottom the most useful type of tackle to use is a standard running leger (fig 29). I find this kind of tackle fishes best when used in a fairly moderate

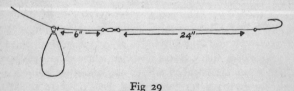

Fig 29

swell, for under these conditions the action of the waves will dig out many edible creatures which will then be swirled about until they manage to find temporary refuge under a flat rock or some other obstruction. The baited hook will also waver about and should appear as a natural object to the feeding cod. Most important of all the line will run through the eye of the weight and the taking fish will be able to move off without feeling the drag of the lead. Cod caught on free-running leger tackle are usually hooked well 'down', a fair indication that they have taken the bait and hook without fear. This is a useful method of catching codling, although it works well with the larger fish as well.

*Paternoster Tackle*

Many tackle dealers still display and sell the old-fashioned wire paternoster. This abomination should have no place in the modern angler's tackle bag, for it belongs to an age of green-

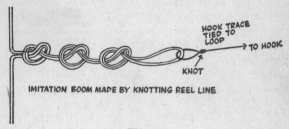

IMITATION BOOM MADE BY KNOTTING REEL LINE

Fig 30

heart rods, deerstalker hats and plus-four trousers. The idea of the paternoster is sound – it is just the wire construction that is outdated; nowadays most shore anglers make their own simple paternosters by knotting their reel line to form an imitation boom (fig 30). The 20 in hook trace is then tied directly to the loop of this nylon boom. This is a style of terminal tackle much used by northern anglers who generally use two-hook tackle (fig 31). The lead is attached directly to the end of the reel line. The first boom is generally 6 to 8 in above the casting weight, while the second is a further 25 in up the line. The hook traces must be the same length otherwise the tackle will tangle. When fishing in a rough sea it is advisable to attach a 2 to 3 in wire extension to the lead (fig 32) so that if it becomes buried in the sand the wire will project above the sea bed and stop the line from fraying as it chaffs through the sand or gravel on the bottom. Two-hook tackle is particularly

Fig 31

useful when fishing for codling, but when large cod are expected, I prefer to use a single hook, because there is always the chance of hooking two fish at the same time, and a pair of big cod pulling against each other stand more than a fair chance of breaking the reel line and escaping.

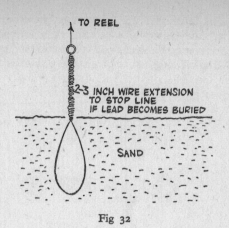

Fig 32

## Rotten-bottom Tackle

Yorkshire cod men habitually fish amongst thick rock and weed. Because of this they expect to lose quite a lot of terminal tackle during a single day's fishing. To minimize these losses they use a local variant of the single-hook paternoster which is called a 'rotten-bottom rig'. This is simply constructed by tying a three-way swivel directly to the end of the reel line: for this tackle the line often has a bs of 60 lb. The lead is then tied to the lower swivel eye by a length of old line which has a much lesser bs than the reel line. The hook snood is attached to the third swivel eye and the tackle is complete and ready for use (fig 33). With this tackle only the lead is lost if the gear becomes snagged up and, more important still, fish that are hooked when the weight is fast in the sea bed can still be landed, for a strong heave with the powerful cane rod will soon break the line between swivel and lead so that the fish can be reeled in safely. This interesting form of tackle is often employed by the intrepid northern cliff anglers, a hardy bunch of men who think nothing of fishing from the top of a cliff in biting winter wind. This is a daring form of angling and is not a method I would advise anyone who has no head for heights

43

to try. The tackle is cast in the normal way, but usually swings back so that it falls directly beneath the cliffs; any fish which are hooked are reeled or hand-lined up the cliff face, and many of course drop off long before they come within reach of the angler.

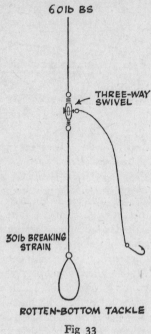

60lb BS

THREE-WAY SWIVEL

30lb BREAKING STRAIN

ROTTEN-BOTTOM TACKLE

Fig 33

*Cod on Artificial Lures*

In Norway and Sweden it is common for shore anglers to use artificial lures for cod fishing. So far this idea has not seriously been adopted in this country although from time to time articles dealing with the subject appear in the angling press. Cod are predatory and there can be little doubt that a shiny artificial lure is a good cod bait. Recently a Kentish angler caught over 500 lb of large cod while spinning from a small boat. Catches like this are unlikely to fall to the shore angler but I quote this as an example of the effectiveness of artificial baits for cod. The ABU company of Sweden market a number of cod lures, one of the best being the 'pirk' pattern. This is a heavy prismatically shaped bait (fig 34) which can be purchased in a range of weights up to 3½ oz. For shore fishing a

PRISMATIC 'PIRK' BAIT FOR COD

Fig 34

pirk bait should be cast out as far as possible and then retrieved at a steady speed so that it flashes along just over the sea bed. I think in future years the value of artificial lures for cod fishing will become recognized by British anglers and no doubt many new and interesting variations on baits and angling techniques will be publicized.

# CHAPTER 4

# Conger

With the development of wreck fishing and the availability of large boats, shore fishing for conger has of recent years dropped out of fashion. This to some extent is understandable, for nowadays most sea anglers are record conscious and as the average size of wreck-caught conger is very very high indeed it is only natural that many anglers are inclined to concentrate entirely on wreck or general boat fishing when they are seeking conger. At the same time it doesn't do to underestimate the potential of shore fishing, for in many areas all round the British Isles deep weedy water can be found within casting range of easily accessible rock ledges and shelves. Providing the ground you fish doesn't dry out completely at low water the chances are that sooner or later a very large eel will be taken from it. It is amazing just how large a conger can be and still live in comparatively shallow inshore waters. A prime example of this must surely be a rock mark known as the Western Rocks which is situated inside the outer harbour wall at Mevagissey in South Cornwall. This comparatively small patch of rocky ground is often alive with conger and several fish in excess of 50 lb have been caught from it at various times. This is the first example that springs to mind but there are many similar marks which if fished constructively would, I am sure, yield fish of similar size.

Several seasons ago when I was fishing various shore marks along the Scottish coastline I was most impressed by the rock fishing grounds on the coast of Wester Ross, and also those of the islands. Conger are by no means scarce in these waters but as yet there are few shore fishermen in this area, consequently the possibilities of this coastline are untapped. With the ever-increasing interest in Scotland as a sea angling centre it is only a matter of time before these grounds are opened up by visiting anglers and when this happens I am sure some mighty conger will be gaffed. In Ireland, where there are a great many rocky areas, conger abound and are caught in such quantity that many shore anglers regard them as little more than a nuisance.

## Size of Conger

The largest conger I can trace was a 250 lb monster caught by a Belgian trawler off the Westmann Islands. I have records also of half a dozen other specimens weighing between 140 lb and 180 lb. Several of these fish were washed ashore dead, their comparatively fresh state indicating that they had not drifted far and had in all probability spent their lives in inshore waters. Eels of these great weights are of course exceptional fish and I only quote them to give some idea of the size conger can attain. The record rod-caught conger weighed 92 lb 13 oz. It is unlikely that this record will stand for much longer for several specimens approaching this weight have been taken from wreck marks during the last year or two and at any moment I expect to hear that a new record eel has been caught. The average weight of shore-caught conger is about 12 lb to 15 lb, fish of this size being very common from rock fishing stations. A 20 lb specimen can be regarded as a good fish, and anything over 30 lb as an excellent catch.

The largest conger I have ever caught while shore fishing weighed 47½ lb but on several occasions I have hooked fish which appeared to be far heavier than this. My 47½-pounder took nearly three-quarters of an hour to land, and the larger fish fought far harder than this. One even broke my specially designed double-built cane rod, then snapped the 80 lb bs braided line I was using. Another large eel put so much pressure on my tackle that it buckled the spindle and reel seat of my big centre pin to such an extent that the reel jammed and I was unable to retrieve or release line. Once this happened the result was inevitable and yet another monster regained its

47

freedom. To be fair I don't even expect to catch or read of a record conger being taken by a shore angler, but I am quite sure that conger of at least 60 lb plus live close to the shore in many rocky areas and although fish of this calibre have all the advantages on their side when it comes to a final battle of strength there is always the chance that a series of lucky moves may bring a really big eel to within comfortable gaffing range. A biggish conger hooked by an angler fishing from a rock mark is far more difficult to control than one hooked from a boat. A boat-hooked fish usually stays directly below the angler so maximum pressure is easy to apply. A fish hooked from a shore mark, however, may be sixty or more yards away from the angler at an angle which makes it almost impossible to keep in direct contact with it. This is another reason why many big conger which are hooked by shore anglers successfully go to ground and eventually break the tackle, for on a long line the fish has only got to alter direction slightly so that the line slackens sufficiently for it to dive under rock or thick weed and the angler is powerless to stop it.

In deep water commercially laid long lines take a steady toll of conger stock. This problem doesn't occur so much in shallow inshore water which is one reason why there are large numbers of decent conger on inshore grounds. At the same time conger are quick to die in cold weather and a sudden icy snap in mid-winter is usually enough to kill off a lot of inshore conger. During the severe winter of 1962–63 thousands of good quality conger perished all round the British Isles but conger are quick to grow and most of the grounds which were denuded of conger during this winter have now been replenished with new stock.

## Location of Conger

Basically, the conger is a rock-haunting fish which spends the bulk of its life in a semi-static position beneath some type of obstruction. In shallow water bare rock seldom attracts these fish in quantity but where the sea bed is comprised of rock and thick beds of tough seaweed conger are usually prolific. Any underwater obstruction providing it is large enough to give the fish shelter should yield good results, but deepish weed-ridden gullies between sharp reefs of rock are usually best. Conger seldom venture out on to open sandy ground during daylight but at night, when these fish begin to hunt actively, it sometimes pays to fish the small sandy coves which abound along most of our rocky coastlines. To get the best out of this sort of fishing the tackle should be cast out so that the bait falls within a yard or two of the weedy rocks. A bait placed like this will often be taken within a few moments of casting. Where the bottom is thick with weed the bait should be cast so that it sinks into the weed. Conger will soon find it no matter how thick the weed growth is.

Rocky ground inside harbour walls is usually a very good place to try and catch conger for the harbour walls offer protection and the fishing boat traffic in and out offers the resident eels an ample food supply in the shape of discarded bait, unwanted fish and oddments of offal. A good many West Country harbours provide good rock fishing marks as do Irish harbours. On the Polruan side of Fowey harbour a series of easily fishable rocks run out from the old fortifications at the harbour entrance. This spot produces many good conger and is typical of the rock marks to which I refer. When choosing a venue for a conger fishing expedition always take careful note of the high water mark and also the layout of the rocks from which you intend to fish. Approached sensibly, rock fishing is safe but accidents can occur, particularly when strong powerful fish like conger are the quarry. Personally I prefer to fish in company when congering, for when it comes to gaffing and subduing even a medium-sized fish two pairs of hands are better than one.

*Feeding Habits and Baits*

Over the years I have caught conger at all times of the day, and at all states of the tide. Conger, however, are basically nocturnal feeders: this is particularly true when one refers to shallow water conger. The optimum feeding period begins at full dark then tails off until the false dawn period during which time conger often indulge in a wild if not prolonged feeding spree. A combination of a warm cloudy night and a rising tide which becomes full two hours or so after dark is the ideal thing for congering. Neap tides are particularly good, for the slack water period of a neap tide lasts far longer than that of a spring tide, and this gives one far more productive fishing time. There are nights which appear to be ideal and which yield no bites at all. This is, however, fairly rare and a warm night and rising tide will normally produce plenty of bites. I once caught two conger which collectively weighed 47 lb during the middle part of a hot summer afternoon. These fish which were taken from a rock mark inside a Cornish harbour caused a great stir among visiting holidaymakers and other spectators. This in my opinion was a most unusual catch and quite exceptional where inshore congers are concerned.

There is a widespread belief that conger are 'filthy' feeders, content to eat any rubbish which comes their way. Putrid fish and offal, for example, are still quoted as being good conger bait which is wrong, for in my experience both as an angler and as a commercial fisherman the only bait that is any good for conger is a really fresh one. Stale baits will occasionally take fish, but for consistently good fishing, fresh baits are essential. Whenever possible I prefer to arrive at my chosen fishing venue early and catch my own bait for congering. Naturally, I also bring herring or mackerel baits with me in case I am unable to catch any bait fish, but more often than not I am successful and land enough small wrasse, pollack and pouting to last for a whole night's fishing. There is a general belief that conger are scavengers which eat only dead fish and crabs which they find among the jumble of rock and weed in which they live. This is far from true for conger are active hunters and catch most of their food alive. Various rock-dwelling fish make up their staple diets, pouting being particularly preferred. Small wrasse and pollack are also taken in fair numbers but pouting seem to attract conger more than any other fish. As bait, pouting should be used within an hour or two of being caught for they are a soft-fleshed fish which decompose very quickly. Conger will eat almost any small fish which come their way, even their own kind, and many of the conger I have opened have contained either whole small conger or the remains of small conger. One monster which I had on a commercially set long line contained another conger which I estimated to weigh 8 lb to 10 lb.

Conger also eat crustaceans, and on many occasions when I have examined the stomach contents of freshly caught specimens I have found remains of crabs and also small lobsters. Hard-backed crabs are usually much in evidence during these examinations, but where the lobsters are concerned I am inclined to think they were eaten while in the process of changing their shells; during this period even a big lobster is incapable of defending itself for it is little more than soft jelly which makes it very vulnerable to attack. Squid is often quoted as being 'the best conger bait' but I am afraid I cannot agree on this for although I have used fresh squid extensively as bait I cannot say that I am over-impressed with it as a fish catcher. The only advantage it does have over fish baits is that it is tough and will remain firmly on the hook. That is the only recommendation I can make where squid is concerned. Conger are greedy fish and where possible I prefer to use big baits on large sharp hooks. Even a 5 or 6 lb conger is capable of swallowing a whole mackerel so why cut a fish bait into sections when it is more attractive and natural used whole? The trouble is, a great many anglers think conger are stupid creatures which will snap at any old chunk of fish. Consequently, it is common to see anglers using a small piece of bait on a big hook, the bulk of the hook being exposed. To expect conger to take this kind of tackle is wrong, for they are cunning fish, quick to eject a suspect bait.

## Conger Behaviour

Although conger have immensely powerful jaws, they tend to be very delicate, fussy feeders. Because of this, many anglers are unsuccessful where conger are concerned; one of the commonest faults being the premature strike. Patience is the answer to this for although it is a great temptation to strike at the first hard pull of a taking fish, more often than not the strike will simply pull the bait out of the conger's jaws, which in all probability will alarm it to such an extent that it will go off the feed for some length of time. By waiting for a feeding eel to start moving away before striking very few fish will be missed, but it is essential to wait and ignore the preliminary 'knocks' which the hungry fish gives. Usually conger bites follow a distinct pattern. First, the fish will pick up and drop the bait a few times. This preliminary investigation of the bait registers as a slow downward drag on the rod tip. At the first indication I usually pick up the rod and feed a few inches of line off the reel so that the eel feels no restriction. These mouthings of the bait normally continue for some time until the eel is sure there is no danger. Having made up its mind to this it will usually start to move away swallowing the bait as it goes. This is the time to strike for once the eel is on the move, a powerful strike against the weight of the moving fish is usually more than sufficient to set the hook deeply into the soft flesh at the back of the eel's mouth. So remember, don't ever strike too soon, for conger like to play and suck at the bait for some time, before attempting to swallow it properly. There are times when although the conger are pulling at the bait, they will refuse to take it properly. This can be most frustrating for although all the preliminary bites are registered, nothing concrete comes of them. The only way I have discovered to overcome this is to use the head of a fish with the guts left attached to the throat and gills of the bait. Cut three-quarters of the way through the bait starting directly behind the gill covers (fig 35), then hold the body of the bait in one hand and the head

FISH HEAD BAIT CUT SO THAT 'GUTS' ARE LEFT HANGING

Fig 35

in the other and gently pull them apart so that the intestines of the bait are left attached and intact to the head. This bait is a killer and will usually tempt the fish to take the bait properly at times when they will only play with a whole fish, or fish fillet bait. Presumably the softness and the flavour of the intestine is the attraction.

There are many old wives' tales which are firmly believed by sea anglers, one of the most ridiculous being the theory that conger won't go for a hard bait, so to be successful soft fillet baits should be used. What absolute nonsense this idea is. Open up any conger and the chances are it will contain whole hard crabs, or quite sizeable fish. Very often these will be wrasse, which are hard, bony fish, covered with a thick coating of tough armour plate like scales. Horse mackerel are also taken freely despite the thick sharp bony ridge which runs along the side of these fish. It's about time that anglers in general ceased to believe most of the traditional nonsense which is continually being repeated by word of mouth or sometimes through the medium of the angling press. The trouble is that so many anglers continue to follow the old ideas and every so often they meet with success and because of these mediocre catches the old beliefs continue to flourish.

## The Conger as a Fighting Fish

Any angler who deliberately attempts to play a good-sized conger in a sporting fashion is courting disaster, for conger are rough and tumble fighters which follow no rules; brute force on both sides is the order of the day, with no holds barred for either contestant. Seldom will conger feed far from some substantial underwater obstruction, consequently a hooked fish must be skull dragged up and away from the bottom the moment it is hooked, otherwise it will snake into a hole or crevice, or hook its tail round some immovable object and slide backwards round the object until it snags the terminal tackle. Once this occurs, the chances of ever landing the fish are very slight and usually a breakage is inevitable. If one is successful in the first instance, and the fish is pulled away from its

53

retreat, then the chances of landing it are good, providing it doesn't manage to get its head down again.

Conger are incredibly strong and fight harder than practically any other big fish on the British List. It is a different sort of fight, however, for seldom if ever will conger make any long runs. Normally they content themselves with slogging it out where they are hooked. One of the most dangerous times in a battle with a big eel occurs when the fish is brought to the surface, for at this stage they tend to revolve at speed and thrash the water into white foam. This is really tackle-smashing action which will soon find any weakness in the reel line, trace or hook, and even when the eel has been gaffed and dragged ashore it is still capable of making good its escape, for unlike the majority of fish which give up at this stage, conger will continue to writhe and twist until they are dispatched with a few good blows to the head and vent. There is nothing pretty about conger fishing. It is at best a brutal bloody affair, which can leave the angler exhausted. At the same time the sheer danger and excitement of fighting a big conger ashore makes it a most worthwhile sport, and in my opinion is one of the most thrilling aspects of sea angling.

## The Luck Element

Sooner or later during his or her career, every regular angler manages to catch a big fish of one kind or another. This is luck. To catch big fish consistently, however, is a different proposition which is easier to achieve with some species than others. Nomadic fish which do not frequent any one area for more than the space of a tide are difficult to catch in quantity and a big one comes by chance with the average run of fish. With conger which take up residence in a given area, the problems are much simpler. For one thing, the fish will usually give its presence away by smashing up various anglers' tackle and providing you take the trouble to check up on the details of these breakages it is usually possible to pinpoint the habitat of the 'tackle smasher' and also draw some conclusions as to the times it can most be expected to feed. Having done this the only thing is to fish the spot hard and consistently with suitable tackle and fresh baits until the big fish is hooked. Most inshore conger marks have their resident monsters which can be caught providing the angler is prepared to put in the time at one venue. Obviously many lesser fish may be caught but more often than not you will get the bigger one within a few days of commencing operations.

## Tackle

As I have already stated there is no finesse about conger fishing and the angler who wishes to fish light should forget about conger and concentrate on other fish. Choice of tackle is to some extent a matter of personal preference. Far too many anglers subscribe to the theory that any old tackle will do for congering which is one reason why so many breakages occur.

## The Rod

Glass has superseded all other rod-making materials and the conger enthusiast has a multitude of suitable rods to choose from. Before purchasing a rod, however, it is sensible to carefully review local venues, then choose the rod accordingly. A good conger rod should be strong yet flexible enough to cast a big bait accurately, and its fittings must be of a good quality and robust, for a conger rod takes a lot of hard knocks over the years and inferior fittings are quick to crack or corrode. For general use an 11 or 12 ft hollow glass beach-caster capable of throwing weights of 8 to 10 oz is the type of rod which I would recommend. These rods are rather expensive, but are well worth the money they cost. Solid glass rods are cheaper but are far heavier and rather tiring to use. If, however, expense dictates the choice of the rod, then a perfectly usable solid glass instrument can be obtained for roughly two-thirds of the price of the hollow glass type. Don't, however, buy a solid glass rod of more than 10 ft in length. Even this size they become rather floppy cumbersome objects difficult to control and use.

## Reels

Only two types of reels are of any practical use for shore fishing for conger; these are the multiplier type and the centre pin. Good quality large-diameter centre pins are difficult to obtain these days, but if one can be purchased they make a first-class conger reel. There are of course plenty of multiplying reels available, but always remember that a conger reel has to hold at least two hundred yards of forty or more pound bs line so when choosing a multiplier make sure the drum is large enough to take the heavy line. Reels with metal spools are best for use with plain nylon lines, for nylon contracts under pressure and will easily crack a plastic spool. This is a point worth bearing in mind. Fixed-spool reels are of no use whatever for conger fishing for although they are easy to cast with, their limited line capacity makes them impractical. The bale arm mechanism is also liable to snap or twist under strains which makes them unreliable when pitted against the brute strength of big conger. For ease of casting both centre pin and multiplying reels need to be carefully cleaned and lubricated after each outing.

## Lines

Conger live among thick jagged rock, the kind of bottom which will quickly wear through line. Because of this I prefer to use plain nylon for conger fishing for even in the heavier breaking strains it is comparatively inexpensive when compared to the braided Terylene lines which are the only alternative. For ease of use the Terylene is superior to the nylon but costs a great deal more. The main drawback with heavy nylon is that it has a natural springiness which makes it a little difficult to control. The braided line is far more supple but doesn't really warrant the extra expense. The only time I use braided line is when I am forced through various circumstances to fish with a line of above 50 lb bs. Normally I find a 40 lb to 45 lb nylon line to be adequate for most of the conger fishing I do.

## Trace Wire

Forty to fifty pound bs nylon-covered braided wire is the best trace material as yet available. This can be bought by the coil and traces can be made up at home. This is cheaper than buying factory-made traces. The beauty of the home-made trace is that it can be made up to suit your own requirements. A special

NYLON COVERED WIRE

BRASS CRIMP

Fig 36

crimping tool and suitable crimps (fig 36) should also be purchased so that the trace can be neatly and securely finished off.

## Hooks

The best conger hooks I have yet used are the flat forged eyed hooks made by Mustads. These are easy to sharpen, have a good penetration and are very strong. Every trace should carry a large swivel; these should be oiled so they move freely under strain.

## How to Make Expendable Weights

Rough ground can claim an awful amount of terminal tackle during the course of an average season's fishing, and these days when all items of tackle are expensive this loss of gear can be a costly business. Lead weights are expensive at the best of times and although most shore anglers use scrap lead to make their casting weights, the metal still costs money and is often hard to come by. Because of this I prefer to use a weight made up from

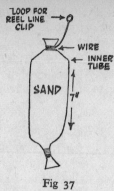

Fig 37

a length of bicycle inner tube, filled with damp sand (fig 37); a 7 in length of inner tube is about right. This should be knotted at one end, packed with sand, and securely wired at the other end. A loop should be left in the wire so that the 'sand bag' weight can be clipped on to a running boom or big buckle swivel. The only drawback to this sort of weight is its overall bulkiness, but as these weights cost nothing to make this slight disadvantage is easy to overlook. The beauty of this type of weight is the fact that it is slightly pliable which makes it less prone to snagging. It also tends to bounce off rock rather than to drop heavily on to it like a lead weight. Better still, expendable weights give you the confidence to fish among the roughest rocks and thickest weed. This is good, for the largest fish usually live among the 'rough stuff' and by fishing without fear of losing more than a hook or a swivel the chances of catching more and bigger fish are much increased.

## CONGER METHODS

### The Running Leger

For general conger fishing the plain running leger rig (fig 38) is best. I find it particularly useful for fishing in deep rock gullies which have a flat or weed-free bottom. Under these circumstances the leger cannot be bettered, but when it is used among thick weed it has a tendency to become entangled with the thick weed stems which almost invariably means the loss of the terminal tackle. The beauty of the leger is that the slightest bite can easily be detected. This is an important point, for

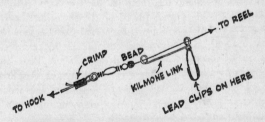

CRIMP
SWIVEL
WIRE
CRIMP
SWIVEL
WIRE
CRIMP

RUNNING LEGER FOR CONGER

Fig 38

conger, particularly the larger fish, are rather shy biters, quick to drop a suspect bait. With the running leger each bite can be easily felt and at each pull a few inches of line can be fed to the pulling fish. Providing the tackle is set up correctly in the first place, this loose line should run easily and smoothly

TO REEL
CRIMP
BEAD
KILMONE LINK
TO HOOK
LEAD CLIPS ON HERE

ARRANGEMENT OF TERMINAL TACKLE SO THAT REEL LINE
CAN RUN OUT SMOOTHLY WHEN AN EEL TAKES THE BAIT

Fig 39

through the lead link (fig 39) and at no time should the fish feel the drag of the lead. There are occasions when conger can be taken on the most clumsy tackle, and I have known conger to drag big leads all over the sea bed and still take the bait, but these are exceptional fish and the angler who wishes to catch plenty of good conger should put plenty of thought into the arrangement of his tackle.

Carelessly assembled tackle leads to poor sport; it always surprises me that so many anglers believe that any old rubbish will do for conger fishing. Worse still, many of these anglers seem to expect to be broken up by every big conger they hook. This is criminal, but I have seen many a good conger with a jaw full of hooks, some of which have caused festering wounds. No one can help being broken up on occasions but to use old and worn tackle when after a big fish like the conger is wrong, and to leave hook after hook in these fish is in my opinion deliberate cruelty. You may think that I am exaggerating this problem, but go to any well-fished area which holds conger and you will hear tale after tale of a monster eel which has broken line after line. Several of these so-called monsters have fallen to my tackle, and on each occasion have turned out to be medium-sized eels weighing between 20 and 30 lb. Good fish, but not exceptional specimens by any means. One such eel which I caught from a Cornish rock mark had eleven rusty hooks in its mouth. The jaw of this particular eel was a mass of inflamed septic flesh and feeding must have been very difficult for it, yet local anglers were proud of the fact that they had hooked and lost this poor creature. This attitude is wrong. Catch fish by all means, but where possible use tackle which is suitable for the species you seek and don't boast about losing fish after fish. There is nothing clever about that. Angling is only clever when fish are landed, so choose and use sensible tackle, otherwise you are condemning living creatures to a life of torment and a slow unpleasant death.

*The Paternoster*

For fishing a live fish bait I prefer a fairly long link paternoster (fig 40) to the more conventional leger. A livebait is almost impossible to control on the leger and will quickly take refuge among thick weed or under a ledge of rock. This cuts down the chance of a hunting conger finding the bait and also leads to snagging of the terminal tackle. With the paternoster this

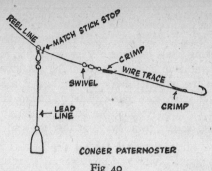

CONGER PATERNOSTER

Fig 40

doesn't occur very often although when fishing rough weed-covered ground some breakages are inevitable, and should be allowed for. Because of the ever-present danger of snagging, terminal tackle should always be kept as simple as possible; at the same time the biting fish should be free to take wire. Be-

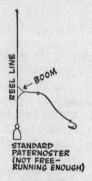

STANDARD
PATERNOSTER
(NOT FREE-
RUNNING ENOUGH)

Fig 41

cause of this the tackle should be set up differently to the standard paternoster which has the lead attached directly to the end of the reel line (fig 41). For conger fishing the hook trace should be attached in this way and the weight tied to a length of nylon complete with swivel. A matchstick clove-hitched to

61

the line makes the stop which holds the tackle together but allows it to run out freely when an eel swallows the bait (fig 42). The nylon trace to which the weight is attached should be of a lesser breaking strain than the reel line so that if the lead does become snagged up only the lead will be lost leaving the remainder of the terminal tackle intact. This is a sound idea, which cuts the cost of lost tackle to the minimum, and may also save you a big fish. Nothing can be more infuriating than to hook a good conger, then lose it because the lead weight has

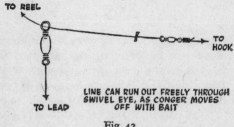

Fig 42

jammed in a crevice. Almost any smallish fish can be used as livebait for conger and there are several ways of hooking these baits to ensure that they stay on the hook during casting and stay alive as long as possible in the water. Hooking the bait through both lips gives a good hook hold, but makes it difficult for the livebait to breathe, and they die quickly. Better methods are to pass the point and bend of the hook through the top lip of the bait, or through the wrist of the tail (fig 43). Surprisingly enough a bait hooked through the tail section of its body will remain lively for long periods of time and appear to suffer little discomfort. Of the two hook holds I have recommended this is the one that I favour most, for I have missed very few bites when using baits hooked in this way, whereas I have found that the lip hooking method sometimes masks the hook and masks the power of the strike.

The angler who decides to use livebait for conger fishing

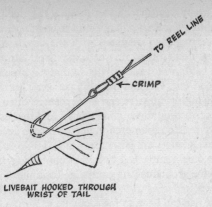

LIVEBAIT HOOKED THROUGH
WRIST OF TAIL

Fig 43

must learn to differentiate between the movement of a lively
bait and the first gentle plucking of a hungry conger. The
difference is fairly easy to distinguish for the movement of the
livebait generally registers as a series of twitches which vibrate
the rod tip. When a conger comes on the scene and pulls at the
bait, a far more definite pull is registered. Although these preliminary bites are by no means sharp, experience will soon tell
you the difference and from then on there should be no bite
detection problem.

*Groundbaiting*

Conger respond well to groundbaiting techniques and the
angler who lives within easy reach of his favourite shore fishing
venue can do well with conger if he carries out a consistent
groundbaiting campaign. 'By 'consistent' I mean distributing
a fair quantity of groundbait over a period of at least three
days before actually beginning to fish. The only thing that can
be used for groundbait is chopped fish. If this can be soaked in
pilchard oil it makes it even more attractive. If the area to be
fished is well covered by water at any state of the tide, then
handfuls of loose fish cuttings can be thrown out and left to

circulate freely round with the flow of the tide. I prefer to use groundbait bombs made up from strong paper bags packed with fish cuttings and weighted with a large stone. These sink quickly but don't break up for some time. More important still, each bag breaks individually so that the groundbait is released at odd intervals and not all together. These 'groundbait bombs' are highly effective and I use them as often as possible, and from re-reading my angling notes I find that on each occasion I have prebaited an area my catches have been far better than normal. Conger are lazy creatures and it doesn't take them long to become accustomed to a free supply of fresh food, and as long as the groundbaiting campaign continues they will frequent the baited area rather than move around hunting for food. Stale fish can be used for groundbait, for the main object is to attract the fish, not really feed them. Under no circumstances, however, should stinking bait be used, and by stinking I mean any fish over a day old.

## Gaffing a Conger

The only practical method of landing a conger is to gaff it, and lift it bodily from the sea in one clean movement. There are many kinds of gaff available, but many are unsuitable for conger, being too flimsy to stand up to the terrific pressures imposed upon them. Extendable gaffs come into the unsuitable category, for although a telescopic handle can be useful, these gaffs lack the necessary strength to deal with a decent conger and either snap or bend under the strain. Remember that a gaffed conger doesn't lie still on the gaff; no such luck – it twists and contorts its body and generally tries to lever itself off the steel hook and only a strong gaff head will stand up under this sort of pressure. I prefer to purchase a gaff head (fig 44A), and lash it securely to a length of stout blackthorn (fig 44B). Having lashed it to the handle as tightly as possible, I then apply several coats of marine varnish to the cord whipping so that the cord contracts and makes a neat, tight, water-resistant job. Blackthorn is the ideal material for a gaff handle, for it is a tough springy wood capable of standing up to heavy

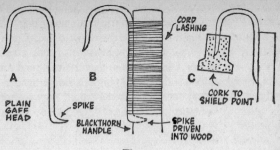

Fig 44

weight without splitting or snapping at a crucial time. The gaff point should be honed to a sharp point and when not in use should be covered by a cork (fig 44C). I like to gaff my conger just behind the head, but other anglers prefer to gaff them through the middle of their bodies. This is a personal choice, but whichever method you use, get the eel out of the water as quickly as possible, for they are quick to lever themselves off a gaff.

*Handling Conger*

Controlling a large eel which is thrashing about on slippery weed-covered rocks is no easy matter, for even a medium-sized conger is remarkably strong and difficult to subdue. Some anglers speak of severing the eel's backbone with a sharp knife, or chopping its head off with a hand axe. Neither method is practical, and the angler who tries these tactics is more likely to seriously injure himself long before he manages to kill his catch. The two items I find most useful for controlling conger are a mallet and a large heavy-duty polythene bag of the type used to hold fertilizer or other compounds. The mallet is the ideal weapon for a conger and one heavy blow on the eel's snout is normally enough to stun it long enough to either extract the hook or cut the trace, and drop the fish into the bag. A sack could be used but the polythene bag is easier to keep clean, an important consideration, for stale conger slime stinks beyond belief. It is always best to go conger fishing with at least one companion for rocks are tricky places to fish from at the best of times, and after dark they are doubly dangerous particularly when fish as large and powerful as conger are the quarry. I have caught a great many conger from rock marks and am used to gaffing and handling big eels single-handed but there have been many occasions when I would have welcomed some help. So be wise and fish with company whenever possible.

# CHAPTER 5

# Mackerel and Garfish

Every sea angler is familiar with the mackerel, for this hard-fighting, fast-moving fish is common all round the British Isles during the summer months. Size for size the mackerel is as game as any fish that swims, and even a medium-sized specimen hooked on light tackle can put up an unbelievable fight before it is subdued. A fresh mackerel is a handsome fish which cannot be confused with any other common species. It has a beautifully proportioned streamlined body. The back varies in colour from a rich blue to a light green. These basic colours are marked with a wavy pattern of dark vertical bars. The sides are silverish-white, and when the fish is first caught they are shot with tints of blue, purple, gold and rose. The average size of rod-caught mackerel is 12 to 16 oz but specimens up to 4½ lb have been caught. Generally speaking, any mackerel over 2 lb in weight can be classed as a good fish. In Scotland the average run of mackerel seems to be a little larger than fish caught around the south coasts of England, and on my last summer expedition to the west coast of Scotland I consistently caught mackerel weighing around the 2 lb mark. These Scottish fish seemed to carry a lot of body fat, probably caused by the abundant food they find in Scottish waters.

There is another kind of mackerel which occasionally finds its way into our seas. This is the colias or Spanish mackerel which closely resembles the common mackerel except that its head and eyes are considerably larger than those of the true mackerel. Colias mackerel reach a weight of around 6 lb. These fish are now rather rare.

Although mackerel are basically summer fish which visit our shores in enormous shoals, I have from time to time caught mackerel during every month of the year, and it is my belief that quite a few of the larger fish take up a permanent residence in inshore waters. In Cornwall these fish are called 'ground mackerel' for unlike the shoal mackerel which tend to feed above the mid-water mark the larger 'ground mackerel', as their nickname implies, spend their life feeding on or very close to the sea bed. During the summer months immense shoals of mackerel come close inshore in search of food. These fish are caught in huge numbers by both the pier and the rock anglers. During the winter months, however, the main shoals make for the deeper water, and only the odd large ground mackerel are left. During the past few seasons vast shoals of mackerel have been located in deep water off the Eddystone Lighthouse and these fish have provided West Country commercial fishermen with good winter fishing. Mackerel make excellent eating and most shore anglers like to catch these fish when they can.

A fish which often arrives a week or two earlier than the summer mackerel shoals is the garfish. Its appearance is considered by many to be a sure sign that the first mackerel catches will soon be made, and a local nickname for the garfish is 'mackerel guide'. Garfish are easy to identify by their long, silver, eel-like bodies and their beaked mouths make them distinctive fish. Even so, newcomers to sea angling who catch their first garfish are often convinced that they have caught some rarity. Although not as powerful as the mackerel an adult garfish is a sporting little fish which puts up a brilliant display of aerobatics before it can be brought ashore. Some anglers regard garfish as vermin, probably because they are widely believed to be uneatable, since when cooked their bones are green. This, like so many angling legends, is rubbish, for in the Baltic garfish are highly prized as table fish. I once caught over seventy large gars at one sitting and the whole lot were eagerly accepted by a party of Danish holidaymakers who were absolutely delighted with them. I must admit that I don't bother to eat garfish myself, not because they are unpleasant, but because they are thin fish and rather difficult to prepare. Sections of garfish make excellent baits for conger and other large pre-

68

datory fish, and cuttings taken from the burnished silver side of a freshly landed gar make fine mackerel, pollack, bream and garfish bait. The garfish like the mackerel is a fish which spends most of its life hunting close to the surface. Its elongated streamlined body is obviously built for speed, and as its appearance suggests the garfish is an active predator which lives mainly by harrying the sand eel shoals. The average length of rod-caught garfish is around 20 in and at this size the fish will weigh less than a pound. On light tackle it is a spectacular and often brilliant fighter, for it will spend almost as much time out of the water as in it. To watch a big garfish walk over the surface on its tail is a thrill for any angler, and I am always pleased when I can try for garfish on light tackle. They seem to be fascinated by floating objects, and a bait cast so that it falls close to a clump of floating seaweed or near to a half-submerged fishbox will usually bring immediate action.

The toothed beak of the gar seems to frighten many anglers, but these fish can be handled easily and without danger. The habit of breaking off the twin beaks of the gar is a stupid brutal habit which far too many anglers follow. It is unspeakably cruel to do this and then return the fish to the sea, to die of starvation, yet every year I see ignorant anglers doing this and laughing at the antics of the maimed fish as it shakes its mutilated head on the surface. Whether or not one likes garfish is immaterial and cruelty of this kind should be suppressed.

A fish which closely resembles the garfish is the skipper or saury pike. It is a smaller species than the gar, seldom attaining a length of more than 15 in. The bill of the skipper is relatively shorter than that of the garfish and the teeth are finer. Both the dorsal and anal fins of the skipper are split up into a main portion and a series of separate finlets, like those of the mackerel. The dorsal and anal fins of the true garfish are not split up in this fashion. The skipper is less common than the garfish. The name skipper is derived from the fish's habit of jumping or skipping over floating objects.

## Optimum Feeding Times

Both mackerel and garfish feed best on warm sultry days when calm seas keep the shoals together. Stormy conditions are seldom any good, for rough seas break up the mackerel shoals into small fast-moving groups which seldom stay in any one area for more than a few minutes. During settled weather both species can be caught at almost any time of the day. Garfish in particular often bite freely during the brightest midday hours. To get the best results, however, the angler should fish early and late, particularly when mackerel are the quarry, for these fish often go on a wild feeding spree for an hour or so after dawn and during the last hour before nightfall. The ideal mackerel fishing combination is a warm still evening combined with a rising tide which becomes full just before dark. Under these conditions huge bags of fine mackerel can often be caught.

## Feeding Habits

Mackerel and garfish are active predators and live by preying upon shoals of lesser fish. In many areas mackerel become so intent on pursuing their food that they throw themselves right on to the shore. At these times almost any bait can be used with success, for a blood-mad mackerel will take any small shiny object it sees. I have known them even to take large bare hooks, and a good bait can be improvised by wrapping a length of silver paper round the hook shank. Garfish are less suicidal than mackerel but there are times when they will snatch at almost any bait which comes their way. I have never known garfish to beach themselves like the frenzied mackerel, for as a general rule garfish like to keep a fair depth of water beneath themselves at all times. I have yet to catch either a mackerel or a garfish while night fishing and I can only draw the conclusion that neither fish feeds much after dark.

## Baits

For float fishing, worm or fish cutting baits are best, of the latter a cutting from the side of a fresh mackerel or garfish being the most deadly. Fish cuttings should be cut carefully with either a thin-bladed knife or a razor blade. To do this properly the bait fish should be laid on a firm flat surface (fig 45A). Normally a bait should be cut crosswise, but if a longer than normal bait is required, a strip cut longways from the side

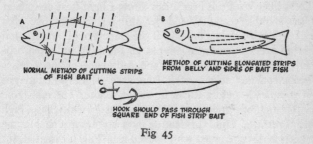

NORMAL METHOD OF CUTTING STRIPS OF FISH BAIT

METHOD OF CUTTING ELONGATED STRIPS FROM BELLY AND SIDES OF BAIT FISH

HOOK SHOULD PASS THROUGH SQUARE END OF FISH STRIP BAIT

Fig 45

or belly of the bait fish should be used (fig 45B). The hook should pass through the square end of the bait, the barb and point protruding from the skin side of the fish cutting (fig 45C). A good many anglers spoil their fish cutting baits by bunching them on the hook. This is wrong, and to fish this kind of bait correctly it should be hooked once only, so that it hangs from the bend of the hook. A bait used in this way will move freely with the action of the sea. A bunched bait will just hang unattractively from the hook. Bait presentation is important, and a bait carefully prepared and thoughtfully used will catch far more fish than one that has been badly cut and lumped on the hook in the belief that anything will do where mackerel or garfish are concerned.

Both fish will take artificial lures freely and any small spoon or plug can be used with confidence. Feather lures are also excellent fish catchers, and the angler who likes to make as much of this tackle as possible can spend many happy hours devising garfish and mackerel lures at home.

Even a monster mackerel would weigh less than 5 lb, and as I said earlier, the average run of both mackerel and garfish weigh less than a pound. Because of this both species can be fished for with ultra-light tackle. My own outfit which I use for both float fishing and spinning consists of a nine-foot hollow glass spinning rod, a fixed spool type reel and a hundred yards of 5 lb bs line. With this gear I can throw a light float or spinner a considerable distance, and yet still feel every move of a hooked fish. Mackerel are one of the gamest of all sea fish and even an average specimen can put up a lengthy and often brilliant battle. The sheer speed and endurance of mackerel is phenomenal and on the tackle I use each fish has to be played out completely before it can be swung ashore. The reel I use for this kind of fishing is an 'Intrepid Classic' which has a high rate of retrieve. I find this feature most useful for it enables me to keep in direct contact with hooked fish. This is essential, for mackerel move at considerable speed and their habit of zig-zagging and doubling back on themselves can lead to lost fish unless direct contact is maintained at all times.

For float fishing with natural baits a size 4 or 6 (freshwater scale) eyed hook is best; for fish baits plain hooks should be used; when baiting with worm, hooks with barbed shanks are

BEAKED HOOK
WITH BARBED
SHANK FOR
WORM BAIT

Fig 46

best (fig 46). For mackerel and garfish small streamlined floats are best, and sliding patterns are the most useful (fig 47). Normally I make my own floats, but suitable patterns can be purchased. A float which requires more than half an ounce of lead to cock it is too heavy for mackerel fishing. Some years ago I made a special float for mackerel fishing. This was designed for long-range work which made for difficult striking. This float was constructed from balsa wood and incorporated a perspex disc (fig 48). This disc turned an ordinary float into

Fig 47

a self-striking float, for as soon as a mackerel or garfish took the bait and dived, the pressure of the perspex disc against the surface drove the hook firmly home. Since then I have used this float for pollack fishing as well and have found that it

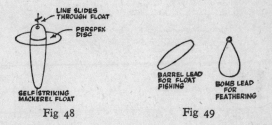

Fig 48                    Fig 49

works splendidly providing the fish take the bait and dive. If they move off across the surface the float doesn't work properly at all. Fortunately both mackerel and garfish normally drag a float straight down as they take the bait, and for long-range work I have found this float to be indispensable. Small barrel leads (fig 49) are the best type of weights to use for float fishing and bomb weights (fig 49) for feathering. A selection of small barrel and snap swivels should be carried at all times.

## Spinning

Both mackerel and garfish respond extremely well to artificial lures and, because of this, spinning is probably the most widely used method of catching both species. Neither fish is fussy about the type of spinner used and any small shiny lure can be employed with confidence. There are dozens of suitable lures adorning most tackle stockists' windows and the spin fisherman is at liberty to choose his own lures. Artificial baits, however, have a strange fascination for most anglers and unless one is careful collecting them can become a mania. This compulsive purchasing of attractive lures is a mistake, for both mackerel and garfish can be caught on the simplest of baits, and beautifully finished expensive spoons are no more than a waste of money, particularly where the shore fisherman is concerned. Sunken reefs and weed beds claim many spinners during the course of a mackerel season, and it is economic to buy cheap lures which are plain yet practical. For example, the old-fashioned mackerel spinner (fig 50) costs very little and yet is a

PLAIN MACKEREL SPINNER

Fig 50

first-class fish catcher. A supply of these should be carried at all times. Plain 2 in type wobbling spoons (fig 51) are excellent lures. These can be obtained in a variety of body thicknesses and for shore fishing the thickest and heaviest are best because

FISH SHAPED WOBBLING SPOON

Fig 51

VOBLEX SPOON

MEPPS
SPINNER

Fig 52

long accurate casts can be made without the necessity of adding extra weights to the line. Voblex and Mepps bar spoons (fig 52) are also good but cost a little more than the lures previously mentioned. When the mackerel are right inshore chasing the brit and other small fry I have often used a small joined plug bait (fig 53) to good effect. These baits are best used when the

SMALL JOINED PLUG
(HOME MADE)

Fig 53

mackerel are shoaling close to the surface. When using a light lure of the traditional mackerel spinner type, extra weight must be added to the line if longish casts are required, for in itself the mackerel spinner is far too light to cast any reasonable distance.

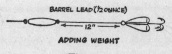

BARREL LEAD (½ OUNCE)

←— 12″ —→

ADDING WEIGHT

Fig 54

I have tried a wide variety of weights, but find the best is a plain ¼ oz or ½ oz barrel lead. This should be stopped by a pair of split shot (fig 54) at a distance of approximately twelve inches from the spinner. A link swivel should be used to join the lure to the reel line (fig 55). Many anglers omit this swivel and then wonder why their lines kink and twist after only a few casts. Heavier lures can be fished without extra weights, but a swivel should be used as a connection between lure and

·LINK SWIVEL·

Fig 55

line at all times. It sometimes pays in fact to make up special spinning traces from lengths of nylon. These should be twelve inches long and should incorporate one link swivel and one plain barrel swivel (fig 56). In this way all chances of line twist should be eliminated. This is important, for a twisted line soon

Fig 56

becomes impossible to use, and more than one angler has had to pack up his fishing early in the day because of this problem. All metal unless specially treated soon begins to corrode in salt water, so after a day's fishing make certain that your lures and swivels are thoroughly rinsed in fresh water, and that each swivel receives a drop of oil. A little time spent doing this will prolong the life of your tackle and save you a lot of future trouble.

Spinning for mackerel and garfish is a simple sport, for the flash of the lure is enough to attract the fish. Because of this a plain steady retrieve should be used. In this way, the spinner will flash steadily back through the water until it is intercepted by a fish. Under normal circumstances, a bait retrieved at the mid-water mark is best, but when the fish can be seen working right on the surface, it pays to speed up the winding-in process so that the lure works just under the surface. A big garfish hooked on top of the water will give a dazzling display of aerobatics, and to watch one of these game fighters turning a series of cartwheels or walking across the surface on its tail is a real thrill to any angler. Mackerel rarely break surface in this fashion, but they can be relied upon to put up a terrific struggle beneath the waves. Spinning is an active pleasant form of fishing, which can produce really good catches of prime eating fish.

*Feathering*

Boat anglers and commercial fishermen use feathers a great deal and immense catches are made with these simple lures. For boat work in deep water, strings of up to fifteen feathers are used, but for shore fishing a simple one- or two-hook rig should be used. Feather lures are easily made up at home, for a mackerel fly is made by whipping two cock hackles to a large hook (fig 57): more elaborate flys can be purchased (fig 57)

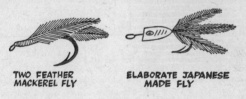

TWO FEATHER
MACKEREL FLY

ELABORATE JAPANESE
MADE FLY

Fig 57

but these are eye catchers and are in no way superior to the normal feathers. Commercially made feathers are sold in a wide variety of colours, red, yellow and green being the commonest. Frankly, I think colour is immaterial where mackerel are being fished for, and nowadays I make up my own lures from plain white or brown hackles, and I still seem to catch as

77

many fish as I did when I used the fancy dyed feather baits. Feather lures work best when employed above a lead. In appearance a set of feathering tackle works is very similar to a conventional paternoster (fig 58), the difference being that feathers catch fish only when they are on the move, whereas paternostering is a static form of angling. Bomb-shaped leads (fig 58) should be used with feather tackle, for these cast

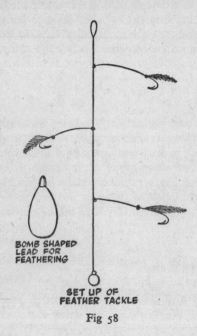

BOMB SHAPED
LEAD FOR
FEATHERING

SET UP OF
FEATHER TACKLE

Fig 58

easily and accurately and don't create too much disturbance while being retrieved. For everyday fishing a ½ oz or ¾ oz bomb is best. When using two feathers it is common to catch two mackerel at a time, particularly when the fish are shoaling.

Anglers are often affected by shoaling mackerel to such an extent that they become greedy and it is common to see anglers using beach-casting rods together with heavy casting weights and multi-feather tackle in order to catch as many fish as possible while the shoals remain within casting range. This type of fisherman tends to talk of his catches in terms of dozens or even hundreds. Mass slaughter of this type is pointless, for who can use a hundred or more mackerel at a time? There is no real sport in this kind of fishing, for the heavy rods and large leads quickly take the fight out of the fish. I find plain two-hook tackle used on light tackle gives me all the fish I require. Moreover, I get fine sport with each fish I hook. Like a spinner, feathers work best when retrieved at a steady rate. To avoid the weight fouling up on the sea bed the rod tip should be kept fairly high (fig 59): in this way the feathers skim along

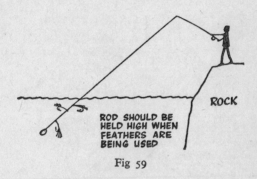

ROCK

ROD SHOULD BE
HELD HIGH WHEN
FEATHERS ARE
BEING USED

Fig 59

around the mid-water mark. Slowing up will usually result in a lost set of terminal tackle so remember to keep the line coming in smoothly and steadily at all times. Mackerel invariably take an artificial lure at such speed that they hook themselves firmly in the process. Because of this it is seldom necessary to strike at a fish as it takes the bait. Garfish are less inclined to hook themselves in this fashion, mainly because the snipe-like bill offers little hold for the hook. The teeth of the garfish, however, often catch across the shank of the hook or the reel line and many gar can be landed without even actually becoming hooked.

## Float Fishing

For the angler who prefers to take things easy, float fishing is the ideal method, for both mackerel and garfish fall readily to float-fished baits and although this is a slower form of angling than spinning, it can still be a most productive technique. Sliding floats are best for this form of angling, and these should be set so that the bait is suspended around the mid-water mark. To make sure the rubber stop doesn't pass through the eye or centre tube of the float it is a good idea to slip a small shirt button on to the reel line between float and stop (fig 60). This will eliminate the problem of the float jamming or passing right over the stop during casting. Some

RUBBER
STOP

SHIRT
BUTTON

FLOAT

TO HOOK
ADDING A SHIRT
BUTTON BETWEEN
FLOAT AND RUBBER
STOP

Fig 60

anglers substitute a bead for the button. This works fairly well, but it must be remembered that a bead is heavier than a button, and if the bead starts to sink before the float reaches it a tangle is almost inevitable. For this reason I find the button method superior.

Mackerel do not always spend their time feeding at the mid-water level, but I find it is best to start at this depth and then adjust the float to raise or lower the bait until contact is made with the fish. Mackerel change their feeding levels quite a lot according to the state of the tide, and when bites suddenly cease, it is best to alter the depth of the float setting until you make contact with the shoal again. Garfish are less inclined to chop and change in this way, and as a general rule the shallower you set the float the more garfish you can expect to catch. On hot calm days I have done extremely well with garfish while fishing the bait at less than three feet beneath the surface. In stormy weather both garfish and mackerel tend to feed very close to the sea bed. Under these circumstances it is best to fish the bait just off the bottom. Sport is very unpredictable during periods of inclement weather, and when the seas are rough I prefer generally to try my luck with other species. For float fishing I use a 4 lb or 5 lb bs trace which is attached to the reel line by means of a barrel swivel. This swivel then acts as a stop for the float, and also stops the line from kinking (fig 61). A 12 in trace is quite sufficient for this type of fishing. Mackerel and garfish are bold-biting fish and the first indication of a bite is usually indicated by the rapid disappearance of the float beneath the waves. Because of this it is essential to concentrate on the float at all times, for unless the strike is made as the float is going down the chances are the fish will throw the bait as soon as it feels the drag of the float. Fortunately, if you miss a fish on the strike it will usually come back and take the bait for the second time. So if a fish has been struck at and missed, leave the tackle where it is and get set for the next pull.

For this sort of fishing, fish strip baits are best for they hang on to the hook well, whereas worm baits are more often than not stripped from the hook by the first bite. For evening fishing, dayglow yellow floats are best, for this colour shows up extremely well in poor light. During the daytime a float with an orange top shows better than any other colour. Strangely enough floats with atomic red tops are difficult to see, and from a distance they look black. Float fishing is great fun, and when fishing from a popular and crowded shore mark it is fascinating to watch the armada of floats as they bob about on the waves.

Fig 61

# CHAPTER 6

# The Mullet

There are four types of mullet in our waters: the small red mullet which is very rare and of no interest at all to the sport fishermen; and three species of grey mullet. These are the thin-lipped, the thick-lipped and the golden-grey mullet, the latter being identified by its golden cheek patches. As far as anglers are concerned all three fish are lumped together under the single title of 'grey mullet'. There are no individual records for these species, the rod-caught record being 10½ lb. This great fish was caught in one of the famous rock gullies around the Isle of Portland in Dorset. This was without doubt an exceptional fish for on average mullet weigh 1½ lb to 3 lb. Anything above 5 lb is a good catch, and anything over 6 lb a specimen to be truly proud of. I have only ever had two mullet over this weight, both being taken from the rocks at Port Mellon in South Cornwall. I have caught a great many fish between 5 lb and 6 lb, however, which lends strength to my theory that mullet over 6 lb in weight are rare fish indeed.

Whether or not a mullet over the record weight will ever be taken it is difficult to say, for although over the years I have watched a great many shoals of big mullet, I can't honestly say I have ever seen a fish which I would estimate to weigh much over 8 lb. Mullet are truly shoal fish, the largest shoals being comprised of the smaller specimens. The very big fish are as a general rule found only in small groups; because of this it is very difficult to catch more than one or two very big mullet at a sitting. With the medium-sized fish, catches of up to a dozen fish are common enough, and even on a bad day it is usually possible to catch enough fish to make a good meal for an average family. Mullet are a southern species which are common from the Essex coast right down to Land's End. They are very common round the Channel Islands and the south-west coast of Ireland. The Channel Island rock marks have produced a good many large mullet over the years, but for the extra-big fish the Portland marks are still some of the best places to fish. In Cornwall, there are many shore fishing marks which produce good catches of prime big mullet, one of my favourites being the big rock that projects into the entrance of Fowey harbour from the Polruan side. Over the years I have taken some very big mullet from this mark and usually catch a good fish or two whenever I fish there. Rock marks at Porthcurno are also very productive – in fact any rocky areas in the south where there is plenty of natural food should be good for mullet fishing. In the natural state, mullet feed mainly on algae and soft mud from which they extract minute aquatic life. Mullet which have been feeding for any length of time on weed usually make poor table fish, for their flesh tastes strongly of weed and mud. Mullet can be classed as scavengers for they are quite happy to suck down almost any edible matter that comes their way. Because of this they can easily be conditioned to take new baits, and a few handfuls of groundbait will soon attract the mullet shoals to a given area.

*Conservation of Mullet*

Mullet are shoal fish and where you find one you will find dozens. Fortunately it is rarely possible to catch mullet in quantity. Consequently it is difficult to seriously deplete the shoals in any one area. At the same time many successful mullet anglers kill all the fish they catch irrespective of whether or not they can use them. This is wrong, for a good many fine sporting fish are destroyed unnecessarily, and indiscriminate killing of this sort should be stopped.

We are living in an age where fish of all types are being caught in vast numbers by commercial fishermen, and also in an age when industrial pollution of one kind or another is rife. Shoaling mullet are particularly susceptible to both these dangers, for they can be netted in huge numbers and, worse still, they have a tendency to feed in rivermouths and harbours where polluted water often takes its deadly toll. Needless to say, most thoughtful anglers are well aware of these problems, but don't seem to realize that by returning a percentage of their catch alive and unharmed to the water they are helping to safeguard their sport in future years. Besides, there is a great deal of satisfaction to be gained from returning a fish alive to its natural element.

The largest catch of mullet I ever made was thirty-five fish at a single tide. These weighed between 3 lb and 5 lb each. Collectively, my catch was extremely heavy, but out of this huge catch I actually retained four fish, which totalled just over 12 lb in weight, more than enough both for me and for my next-door neighbour. The remainder of this catch were put back into the sea as they were caught. Freshwater anglers have learned the value of conservation and sea anglers too must now follow this lead because it won't be long before many of our fish will start to become scarce, and the sooner all anglers realize they can help to preserve these fish the better things will be.

Shoaling mullet are very easy to foul hook, and in a good many places so-called anglers make a regular practice of snagging these fish on a weighted trace carrying two or three large treble hooks. Many of the fish foul hooked in this manner manage to tear free of the hooks, and are left to die with gaping wounds in their backs, sides and bellies. I am afraid to say that this practice is on the increase.

## TACKLE

Mullet fishing is a very specialized form of angling, and there can be no question of employing standard sea fishing tackle when mullet are the quarry. To justify the expense of a complete outfit which can only be used for one type of fish calls for a lot of thought and the angler who decides to purchase such an outfit should be prepared to put it to good hard use at every possible opportunity. Fortuately, mullet fishing is a branch of angling which quickly becomes an obsession and most people who take up this sport tend to become rather fanatical about it. This is very understandable, for mullet are at best a difficult species to catch and, because of this, the challenge these fish present to the average angler is so great that he looks upon each fish landed as a great personal achievement. Anyone who has never experienced the frustrations of mullet fishing may find this difficult to understand, but the fact remains that mullet fishing is completely different to all other forms of sea fishing and the angler who gains enough knowledge to take mullet consistently is a real angler.

To catch these wily fish great patience, skill and angling knowledge is essential and it takes a clever fisherman to overcome the many problems which surround mullet fishing. Probably the most frustrating thing about grey mullet is the way that they shoal in large numbers and show themselves readily to the angler and at the same time refuse to take the slightest notice of the baited tackle. This behaviour is more than enough to drive many anglers away to less difficult fish, which is understandable – for to fish an area which is alive with visible big fish and still catch nothing can be infuriating beyond belief. There are occasions, of course, when a mullet shoal will go mad, and at these times the fish will bite wildly at baits presented on really crude tackle. This is a very rare occurrence, and as a general rule only the lightest of gear should be employed. Even with ultra-light tackle a good many fish will manage to shake free of the hook, for the mullet's mouth is very soft indeed and will tear very easily under pressure. I have tried many ways to overcome this unfortunate problem but as yet I have still to find any true solution, and like most mullet fishermen I have resigned myself to losing a fair percentage of the mullet I hook.

Mullet grow to a good weight and fight as well as bass of similar size. Consequently, breakages also occur from time to time and I would say that any angler who lands one out of every three mullet he hooks has reason to congratulate himself on his achievements. This may sound like a very low ratio of landed fish, but I would say it is a fairly accurate estimate if a seasonal record is kept. When selecting an outfit especially for mullet fishing bear all these things in mind and go to a tackle shop which stocks freshwater gear, for it is among this kind of tackle you will find the ideal mullet fishing rods, reels and lines, etc.

## Rods

During the past season or two many cheap glass spinning rods have found their way into British tackle shops. A good many mullet enthusiasts have wasted money on these rods, for although they are cheap to buy and quite serviceable for mackerel spinning from boats, they are too short and too stiff for any form of mullet fishing. This type of rod is seldom more than 7 ft long, and in my experience the minimum length a mullet rod should be is 10 ft. Remember that it is almost impossible to cast float tackle accurately with a short rod, nor is it possible to strike properly at a taking fish, or for that matter to control a hooked fish correctly. With a long rod these problems do not occur, and although a long rod costs more than a short spinning rod, it is worth every extra penny. The ideal rod to go for is a two- or three-piece hollow glass trotting rod of the type used by Thames and Avon anglers. These rods are designed to cast and control light float tackle easily and yet still have the backbone to lay out a really big fish under difficult conditions. Rods of this type cost between £5 and £10, and like most things you get what you pay for – but bear in mind that all these rods are made for freshwater use and the fittings are not anodized to protect them from the corrosive action of salt water or salt spray, so no matter how much you pay for such a rod, you should always wash it off thoroughly with fresh water after each trip and then wipe it over with a soft rag soaked in machine oil. By doing this religiously the rings and fittings will last for years. Neglect this job, however, and the rod fittings will rust out in a few months, and replacing them can be a costly job, even if you do it yourself.

My own mullet rod has a soft easy action reminiscent in many ways of a fly rod. This particular rod will handle all types of light terminal tackle with ease, and accurate casting is a simple operation. Split cane rods should not be used in salt water.

## Reels

For close-range fishing a freshwater centre pin with a freely revolving drum is a pleasure to use, but for long-range fishing and general use a medium-sized fixed-spool reel is the best type. The slipping clutch mechanism of this kind of reel is invaluable for mullet fishing, for providing this clutch is set correctly so that the reel spool will revolve under the pull of a running fish, the problem of 'smashed' tackle can be minimized. This problem can never be truly eliminated, for a big mullet takes off like a scalded cat as soon as it feels the hook strike home, and the resulting jerk can easily break a light line. I usually set my clutch well below the breaking strain of the reel line; this gives me a little more chance of avoiding a breakage in the initial stages of the fight. As the hooked fish weakens I gradually tighten the clutch up so that I can bring the fish into the waiting net. Once the fish has been landed, unhooked and disposed of, the next job is to re-adjust the clutch so that it can slip under the pressure exerted by the next mullet. Never crank the reel handle while a fish is making the spool revolve. This kinks the line very badly and may weaken it to such an extent that it will snap under very little strain. I give this warning for it is a common fault among anglers and it could lose you a record fish. Hold the reel handle by all means but never turn it while the reel spool is slipping under clutch pressure. Reels, lines and rods should be thoroughly cleaned after each outing, for salt water is dangerous to any unprotected metal, and sand has a habit of getting inside a reel at an alarming rate.

## Line

For all forms of mullet fishing a 4 lb bs monofilament line should be used. This may sound very light for sea fishing, but remember, first, that mullet of all sizes are quick to notice a thick line, and, secondly, that the ideal mullet rod is designed to handle lines of approximately this bs. Almost any well-known make of line will suffice, and most manufacturers give a wide choice of line colours in each individual breaking strain. Pale blue or green lines seem to be best for mullet fishing, and the darker colours are best left alone. One of the first things I do whenever I float fish for mullet is to thoroughly grease the line so that it floats on the surface. This makes for faster, easier striking although in some ways a floating line can be more difficult to control than a sunken one, particularly on windy days when the line has a tendency to 'bag' and drag the float away from the right area. This is only a minor problem, and a floating line is in my opinion essential for most forms of mullet fishing. Most tackle shops stock a good brand of line grease, and a single tin should, barring accidents, last two or three seasons.

*Hooks*

Hooks are legion and even the fussiest of anglers should be able to find a hook which suits his mullet fishing requirements. Remember always that sea hooks are too large and too thick in the wire for mullet fishing, but there are of course plenty of freshwater hooks which suit this form of fishing. Personally I like to use size 12 or 14 hooks already mounted on a 2½ to 3 lb nylon trace. These are neater than eyed hooks of a similar size, and are therefore less noticeable to the fish. Many anglers who have never tried their skill with mullet may think that I am overestimating the cunning of these fish; this is far from the truth, however, for by anyone's standards mullet are cautious, shy creatures, quick to notice anything odd about a bait, and quicker still to fade out of an area in which they sense danger. To save money, eyed hooks can be used, and the best I have found are size 16 goldstrike hooks, or size 12 Sealey Speed Barb hooks. Both are easily obtainable. In my opinion, however, the hook to nylon, with its neatly whipped shank, is superior to either of these hooks.

*Floats*

I consider a selection of floats to be an essential part of my mullet fishing equipment. None of the floats I carry are designed for sea fishing, and many are simply painted bird or porcupine quills. Like all the other terminal equipment, floats should be kept as small and as streamlined as possible. For close-range work, two to three shot quills are ideal, while for long-range fishing I find a slim cork- or balsa-bodied trotting type float (fig 62) more useful. These floats should be attached

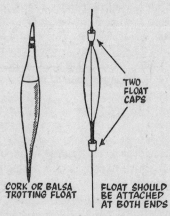

TWO FLOAT CAPS

CORK OR BALSA TROTTING FLOAT

FLOAT SHOULD BE ATTACHED AT BOTH ENDS

Fig 62

at both ends by means of two rubber float caps (fig 62), then if a change of float is called for it is a simple operation to substitute one float for another without breaking down all the terminal tackle.

*Additional Tackle*

A box or two of BB split shot and a dozen very small barrel swivels should always be carried. A coil of fine lead wire is also useful. For paternostering a selection of pear-shaped leads ranging from $\frac{1}{4}$ oz to $\frac{3}{4}$ oz should also be carried. Always make sure that you have plenty of leads, swivels, hooks, etc, for it is easy to lose quite a few during a day's fishing and unless you have enough to carry on with, you might find that you will have to stop fishing simply because of one small item of equipment.

## Landing Mullet

A standard landing net is the best implement to use for landing any mullet you catch. Under normal circumstances the ordinary four foot long handle is sufficient, but when fishing from high rocks, an extendable handle can be an asset. These give an overall length of 8 ft which should be long enough to overcome most landing problems. Take great care, however, to ensure that the locking joint on the net handle is kept clean, well oiled and free from corrosion.

## Best Times of Day

To be really successful with mullet the angler must be prepared to get up well before dawn so that at the first sign of light he can start fishing. Obviously state of tide must be taken into consideration, but as most rock and harbour marks hold plenty of water even at low tide, one should plan to fish as early as possible. The ideal circumstances where first light coincides with half tide only occur on a few occasions during a season, but providing there is enough water to cover the bottom, the mullet will come nosing in over the rocks as the sun starts to rise. If the area has been thoroughly groundbaited beforehand, then sport can be expected straight away. If not, then the fish should be encouraged to feed by the liberal use of groundbait, which should be thrown in at regular intervals. I have caught mullet at all times of the day, but my best results have always been obtained during the first few hours of daylight. As yet, I have never caught mullet after dark although on several occasions when I have been catching fish in the late evening, I have stayed on in the hope of further sport. I don't know why mullet don't appear to take hook baits after darkness has fallen, for the fish are often most active at night, and in my commercial fishing days I would regularly net mullet during the night.

## Mullet Baits

By nature mullet are soft-mouthed sucking fish which live by extracting minute food particles from the soft mud and weed upon which they feed. They are quick to accept new types of food but no matter what they eat they still suck rather than bite at a bait, and their natural inclination is towards soft foods. There are many baits which can be used to catch mullet, some of which require special preparation. The most important of these baits will be listed in this section. To simplify the bait problem, each individual bait will be fully described and its preparation thoroughly explained.

## Bread Baits

Bread in one form or another has accounted for many of the largest mullet yet caught in the British Isles. Because of this, it can rightly be regarded as a top bait, and one which every mullet angler will be well advised to experiment with. The simplest and easiest type of bread bait to use is flake. Flake is the name given to the moist inside of a new loaf. To bait a hook with flake, a portion of bread the size of a thumbnail should be pinched from the inside of the loaf, then folded round the shank of the hook. Only the bread round the hook shank should be squeezed, so that the portion that covers the

PINCHED AREA

SOFT FLAKE

BAITING UP WITH BREAD FLAKE

Fig 63

bend and point of the hook remains ragged and soft (fig 63). This is important, for if the whole bait is compressed, it will harden in the water to such an extent that it will mar the penetration of the hook when the strike is made. Flake is comparatively heavy and can be cast quite well on floatless leadless tackle. Once in the water, it sinks slowly and naturally and is most attractive to mullet.

## Bread Crust

Very occasionally mullet feed or can be induced to feed right on the surface: when this occurs bread crust can be a deadly bait. The best crust comes from a day-old tinned loaf. Some anglers make a habit of cutting their crust baits into neat cubes, but personally I prefer to tear my baits manually from the loaf so that each separate bait appears as natural as possible to the feeding fish. When big mullet are known to be in the area, a piece of crust the size of a 2p piece can be used, but for medium-sized fish, a piece half that size will suffice. In its natural dry state, crust is too light a bait to cast any distance, but weight can be gained by 'dunking' the crust gently in the water before making the cast. Crust fishing is a most exciting way of catching mullet, for being a surface bait, every movement of the feeding fish can be clearly watched, from the first preliminary inspection of the bait to the moment when the crust is finally sucked down. This can be a heart-stopping business, which will leave even the most experienced mullet angler feeling a trifle weak at the knees.

## Bread Paste

Bread paste is a first-class bait for mullet, and one which has brought me a great deal of success. Many anglers experience difficulty in making good bread paste for it takes experience to make a paste that is neither too hard nor too soft. The best paste is made from the crumb or flake of day-old loaf. Tinned loaves are best, for it is easy to remove all traces of crust from these. This is important for I find that paste

93

which contains crust breaks up quickly when immersed in water. Having prepared the bread by removing the crust, the next step is to break the crumb of the loaf into two equal sections. Now soak one half in fresh water, until it is thoroughly saturated. Work this thoroughly through the fingers to get rid of any excess water, then gradually knead the dry bread in with the wet bread. This mixture must be thoroughly worked until a smooth soft paste is achieved. This should be made so that it is strong enough to adhere to the hook during casting but soft enough to pull off the hook when the strike is made.

Having made enough for a day's fishing, the paste should be wrapped in a clean white cloth, so that it can be transported without drying out too much, and picking up too many dirt particles en route. Plain bread paste can be flavoured or coloured to personal choice; the addition of a little custard powder, for example, turns the plain white paste yellow: and honey, cheese, fish paste, or pilchard oil can be added to give the bait a distinctive flavour. I know many anglers who go to extreme lengths to add to the attractiveness of their paste baits, but although I have used coloured and flavoured paste on many occasions I have never found it any better or, for that matter, any worse than plain bread and water paste. If, however, you feel more confident when using a specially prepared paste, then use it by all means, for confidence in the bait is nine-tenths of the battle.

*Cheese Bait*

On several occasions I have caught good-sized mullet while using cubes of soft cheddar or processed cheese. Cheddar seems to be a better fish catcher than the white processed cheese, but both have taken their fair share of fish, and a flat box of processed cheese is easy to carry and keep fresh, and it makes a good standby bait.

*Minced Meat*

I first started using raw meat baits to catch mullet while fishing at a spot where a pipe from a local abattoir emptied

94

directly into the sea. Later I experimented at other venues and found that minced raw meat made a good general bait. Minced meat can of course be bought directly from most butchers' shops and a pound of this is more than enough for a day's fishing.

## Banana Bait

Another soft bait which mullet seem to like is banana. I can give no explanation for this and can only presume that the combination of colour, smell and softness is the thing that attracts mullet to banana-baited hooks. My old friend John Affleck of Golant, Cornwall, introduced me to banana baits for mullet fishing, proving the deadliness of this bait by catching a bag of mullet which included a magnificent 6¼ lb specimen. All these fish were caught from the rocks on the Polruan side of Fowey Harbour. Later we successfully used banana baits while mullet fishing at other stations on the South Cornish coast. Baiting up with banana can be a little tricky at first, but once the knack is obtained it is simple enough. Banana is very soft and the strike should be made at the slightest sign of a bite otherwise the fish will quickly suck the hook clean.

## Worm Baits

Very thin harbour ragworm make fairly good mullet bait. They are, however, rather messy to dig and use, for harbour mud has a glue-like consistency and an indescribable smell. Harbour rag are very soft and break easily when being placed on the hook. Sections of large ragworms are ideal when used in conjunction with mullet spoons (see spinning section of this chapter).

## Maggots as Bait

Freshwater anglers use maggot baits to catch a wide variety of fish, and although I have never given these grubs extensive trials as sea bait, I have used them several times to catch average-sized mullet. Maggots can be bought from many tackle shops, and a plentiful supply can be purchased quite cheaply. As bait maggots can be used either singly or in twos or threes (fig 64). From the diagram readers will see that these grubs

MAGGOTS HOOKED
LIGHTLY THROUGH
THE SKIN

Fig 64

are hooked through the skin on the square end of their bodies. This ensures that they stay lively on the hook, and leaves the hook point and barb free to catch in the mouths of any mullet which take the bait. When maggots are used as bait it pays to throw the occasional handful of loose grubs into the water as groundbait. Maggots are best fished on float tackle.

*Fish Baits*

Small cubes of fish flesh make excellent mullet baits, particularly in areas where fish offal is dumped in any quantity. Oily-fleshed fish like herring or mackerel make the best baits. Care should be taken with fish baits for mullet are very fussy, and in my experience I have found that they will ignore a fish bait that has the slightest vestige of skin adhering to it. Flesh taken straight from a dead fish is often too soft to use straight away. To overcome this problem, bait-sized sections of flesh should be cut, then left to dry in the sun for an hour or so before use. This toughens up the flesh so that it is comparatively easy to keep on the hook. As I said earlier, great care should be taken to ensure that all skin is removed from the bait before use, otherwise negative or at best very poor results will be achieved.

## Macaroni Bait

During 1968 I carried out a series of experiments with baits which I had never tried before. One of these baits which proved to be highly successful on numerous occasions was macaroni. In its ordinary uncooked state, of course, macaroni is of no use whatsoever, but boil it for a few minutes in sugar-sweetened water and it becomes a clean, easy to use, and a very deadly bait indeed. Small sections about an inch long are just about right. These I use on a size 14 hook and float tackle. While at Fowey one year I landed a number of good mullet on this bait and have every confidence in recommending it to other mullet anglers.

## Green Peas

This was another bait which proved to be successful and although I can't say that I would prefer peas to other baits, I have proved to my own satisfaction that they are a useful bait. Peas should be cooked as though for table use. This makes them soft enough to appeal to the mullet and tough enough to stay on the hook during casting.

## Groundbait and Mullet

The most consistently successful mullet specialists all use large quantities of groundbait to attract and hold the attention of the mullet shoals. Mullet are quick to learn about groundbait and always seem prepared to sample any odd food scraps which come their way. A prime example of this is the way harbour mullet quickly learn to feed on bread scraps, most of which which are the remains of holidaymakers' picnic lunches, which have been casually thrown into the harbour as food for the gulls. Quite recently I watched a shoal of medium-sized grey

mullet jostling each other about in the inner harbour at Mevagissey, the cause of their excitement being a handful of loose
bread crust which a visitor had just thrown into the water.
Harbour mullet have every opportunity to grow accustomed
to unlimited supplies of free food, but the mullet shoals that
live and feed round the average shore fishing marks have to be
carefully conditioned before they will come to a groundbaited
area, and even when they do arrive at such a place, they are
quick to show fear at any sign of danger or rapid movement.
This is very understandable, for mullet shoals that live and
feed in isolated areas are not used to the sight of human beings,
whereas the scavenging shoals of harbour mullet soon become
accustomed to the pointing hands and constant movement of
the holiday crowds.

There are a great many ways of using groundbait to attract
mullet, one of the best methods being to prebait a gully at
the bottom of the tide so that as the water rises a constant stream
of groundbait particles are washed out to attract the fish. To
prebait a gully in this way I use a thick mixture of bran,
chopped fish flesh and pilchard oil. This paste should then
be rammed into rock crevices on both sides of the gully. I do
this in stages starting at the low water line and finishing at
the high water mark. In this way the rising tide is constantly
washing out a stream of food particles. By doing this correctly
the attention of the mullet can be held right up until the
slack period at the top of the tide, a time when I find mullet
have a natural tendency to stop biting and disappear. I quite
frequently use ten or twelve pounds of groundbait when pre-
baiting a gully in this way, for I feel it is better to overdo it
rather than skimp on groundbait when mullet are the
quarry.

Another useful method of groundbaiting a rock gully is the
one I call 'the suspended fish strip technique'. This consists
simply of a length of fine string which has a stone tied to one
end and a crab pot cork to the other. In between are tied
half a dozen herring or mackerel fillets (fig 65) each of which
has been thoroughly soaked in pilchard oil. The stone serves
to anchor this string while the buoyancy of the crab pot cork

holds the fish fillets up so that the groundbait string extends from the sea bed upwards. Mullet love to suck and nibble at this sort of attractor, and providing small cubes of fish flesh are used as bait, catching fish should present no great problem. A similar technique which is useful for fishing in shallowish water is the anchored crust method of groundbaiting

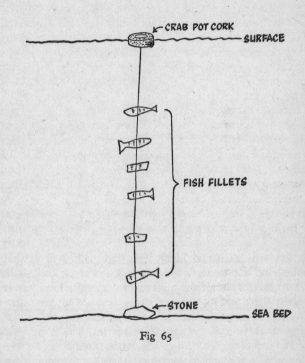

Fig 65

(fig 66). This works on the same principle as the fish string, except that a quarter of a tinned loaf is substituted for the crab pot cork; the bread, being buoyant, floats on the surface while the stone on the other end serves to anchor it in one position. Once mullet learn that bread is good to eat, they often become almost completely preoccupied with it, and it can be quite a heart-stopping sight to watch a shoal of very big mullet mouthing hungrily at the floating crust.

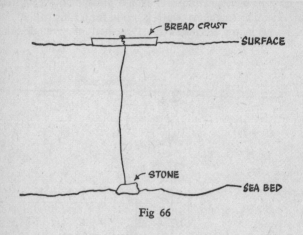

Fig 66

## METHODS

### Float Fishing

This is a pleasant and highly effective method of catching mullet, and one which is very suitable for use against mullet in harbours. By sea fishing standards, a mullet outfit is extremely light, and many anglers who are used to using heavy rods and large sea floats may find it difficult to adapt themselves to the use of the river type tackle which is necessary for all types of mullet fishing. This is understandable, for when one has been accustomed to casting floats which take anything up to an ounce of lead to cock, the delicate art of casting a tiny two- or three-shot float is difficult to master. Practice makes perfect, and once one becomes used to the lightness and delicacy of the outfit, accurate casting becomes easy. Mullet are a species which continually change their feeding depths. One day they feed hard on the bottom and the next they will only look at a bait presented on the surface or at mid-water. With float tackle it is easy to adapt to these changes and although there are many ways of catching mullet, float fishing is still about the best all-round method. Unless the fish are feeding right on

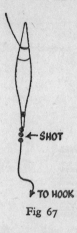

← SHOT

↓ TO HOOK

Fig 67

the bottom, it usually pays to bunch the shot directly under the float (fig 67) so that the bait sinks by its own weight alone. I have always found mullet respond extremely well to a bait which drops naturally down through the water in this way, and because of this I have made many of my mullet floats self-

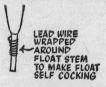

LEAD WIRE
WRAPPED
←AROUND
FLOAT STEM
TO MAKE FLOAT
SELF COCKING

Fig 68

cocking by wrapping a suitable length of lead wire round the base of each float (fig 68). The bunched shot do the job just as well but a float that has been properly weighted is easier to use, and the possibility of weakening the reel line by pinching on split shot has been completely eliminated. If the fish are feeding right on the bottom of course it will save time if the bait is made to sink as fast as possible. Under these circumstances the shot can be placed some six inches from the hook (fig 69).

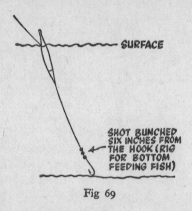

SURFACE

SHOT BUNCHED
SIX INCHES FROM
THE HOOK (RIG
FOR BOTTOM
FEEDING FISH)

Fig 69

In a normal sea, ordinary quill or cork on quill floats should suffice, but when the water is a little choppy then a long antenna float (fig 70) can be used to good advantage. These floats should be weighted so that just the tip protrudes above the surface (fig 70). The body of the float acts rather like the keel of a yacht and helps to stabilize the float. This type of float is amazingly steady in the water and will ride easily over quite rough seas.

Mullet bites vary a great deal, depending upon the depth at which the fish are feeding and also upon the shotting arrangement used to cock the float. When the fish are right on the bottom and the shot are close to the hook, the bite is usually registered as either a sharp bob or a savage pull which causes the float to disappear completely. With surface-feeding mullet where the bait is allowed to fall slowly through the water the bite is normally indicated by the float tipping over to one side before being dragged off across the surface. No matter what kind of bite is given the strike should be made the instant the float starts to move, for as a rule the bait will

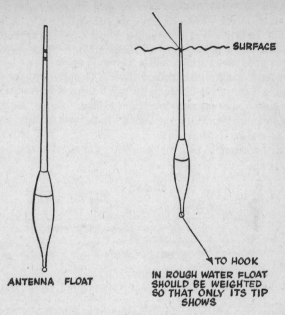

SURFACE

ANTENNA FLOAT

TO HOOK

IN ROUGH WATER FLOAT
SHOULD BE WEIGHTED
SO THAT ONLY ITS TIP
SHOWS

Fig 70

be soft and any delay in striking will give the mullet time to suck the hook clean and depart. To achieve even moderate success while float fishing requires good reflexes and a sharp eye. Even then, a good many bites will be missed completely, and even when fish are being hooked regularly many will manage to shed the hook before being netted, for the soft mouth of the mullet tears very easily under pressure.

## Surface Fishing

In well-sheltered rock gullies and harbours where the water is affected little by wind or tide action, the mullet shoals will often rise to the surface and laze in the warmth of the sun. Under these circumstances they can seldom be induced to look at a bait presented on normal tackle and the only way I have managed to take fish under these conditions is by surface fishing for them. This is a technique which I used a great deal when fishing in lakes and ponds for carp and it has since stood me in good stead while mullet fishing. The only bait which truly lends itself to this method is bread crust, and wherever I locate a shoal of basking mullet my first thought is to scatter a few loose crusts on the water as groundbait. Mullet seem to have an inbred curiosity which makes them want to inspect any edible-looking object which comes their way, and although the first reaction of the shoal is to scatter in alarm as the crusts

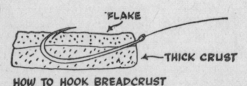

**HOW TO HOOK BREADCRUST**

Fig 71

drop on the surface the fish soon return to sample the bread. A shoal of mullet can clear up quite a lot of groundbait in a remarkably short space of time, and once the fish begin to gulp down the loose crusts the chances of catching a few fish are very high.

For surface fishing no floats or weights of any kind are required, just a rod, reel, line, hook and bait. Even a smallish piece of crust makes a fairly bulky bait, and for this form of fishing I use a size 8 or 10 hook. Baiting up with crust requires practice, and the simplest method is to push the hook through the crust, turn it and push the hook point and barb through again (fig 71). This will hold the bait firmly on the hook during casting and yet leave the hook point and barb masked so that when a fish takes the bait the strike should easily set the hook into its lips. This is a most exciting form of fishing for, having cast the bait out, every movement of the feeding fish can be clearly seen and as they approach the bait tension mounts to an almost unbearable degree. Generally one fish will single out the bait and come for it. If this happens, then there should be little problem in timing the strike, but there will be occasions when a whole gang of mullet will converge on the bait together. Then it is difficult to ascertain whether the crust has been taken or simply sunk by the jostling fish. The only way of finding out is to strike as soon as the bait disappears. Unfortunately there is always the chance of foul hooking fish by doing this, but this is a chance which will have to be taken.

Generally speaking, there is little likelihood of catching a quantity of mullet on surface baits, for the fish are more wary than usual when they are close to the surface, and I normally find that after two or three fish have been taken the shoal tends to disperse for the rest of the day. Surface fishing is without doubt the most exciting form of mullet fishing although not the most productive, but a few good fish taken in this way give me more personal satisfaction than twice the number caught on other techniques and whenever the opportunity occurs, I make a point of using the floating crust method.

## Pasternoster Tackle

When mullet are bottom feeding in water too deep for comfortable float fishing, a light paternoster is the only practical form of terminal tackle to use. Most sea anglers use two- or three-hook paternoster rigs, but personally I prefer to employ only one hook, particularly when mullet fishing, because two hooked fish, both fighting for their lives, can easily smash the ultra-light lines which I normally use for catching mullet, and even if they don't break the line their combined strength will usually tear the hooks out of their mouths. For these reasons I find a single-hook rig ideal. All anglers have a tendency to use complicated terminal tackle, but for mullet which are line shy at the best of times the simpler the gear the more fish it will catch. I make up my paternoster on the spot by sliding a tiny barrel swivel on to the reel line and stopping it some 12 in to 15 in from the end of the line by means of a dust shot. Next I tie a 9 in length of 3 lb bs nylon line to the open eye of the swivel and attach a suitable-sized eyed hook to the end of this trace. Finally the whole rig is finished by a ½ or ¾ oz weight which is tied to the end of the reel line. This paternoster (fig 72) is both simple and effective and is ideal for deep water work.

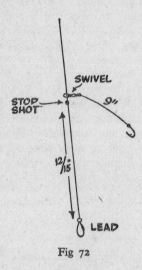

Fig 72

Bread paste or chunks of fish flesh make the best baits for paternoster work. A paternoster is only effective if the line between rod tip and lead is kept as taut as possible (fig 73) so that the bait is kept suspended just above the sea bed. To detect bites, a loop of line should be held in the left hand, and at the same time the rod tip should be carefully watched. At the slightest pull on the line or rod tip, the strike should be made. Any delay will mean a missed fish and a lost bait. Paternostering is a very sensitive method and as there is a direct contact between rod tip and tetrminal tackle few bites should be missed on the strike.

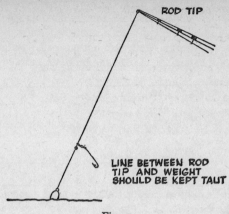

ROD TIP

LINE BETWEEN ROD
TIP AND WEIGHT
SHOULD BE KEPT TAUT

Fig 73

## Spinning

Spinning for mullet is a comparatively new sport, which I believe originated at Christchurch in Hampshire where local anglers devised the method to catch shoaling mullet in the estuaries of the rivers Avon and Stour. Later this method moved westward to Plymouth and although as yet only a very few anglers use this technique it can be looked upon as a very deadly style of fishing. Nowadays proper mullet spoons can be purchased from most tackle shops. These are simply tiny bar spoons mounted in the same way as a flounder spoon (fig 74). The single hook which trails behind the spoon blade should be baited with either a small ragworm, or a section

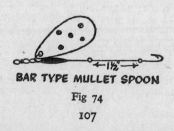

BAR TYPE MULLET SPOON

Fig 74

from the tail of a large ragworm (fig 75). These baits work on exactly the same principle as the flounder spoon, and presumably mullet regard it as a small fish which is making off with a juicy worm. Mullet are not normally predatory but the sight of a baited spoon seems to infuriate them to such an

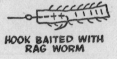

HOOK BAITED WITH
RAG WORM

Fig 75

extent that they throw caution to the wind and make a fast and savage attack on the bait. On the occasions I have used the baited mullet spoon I have never returned home empty-handed, which proves to me that this rather new and novel technique has much in its favour. As might be expected quite a lot of the fish hooked on the spoon invariably manage to tear free, but these losses are something every mullet angler should learn to accept as inevitable.

## The Suspended Leger

The suspended leger is a method which I first saw being used from high rocks at Porthcurno. The angler in question was used to fishing from a south coast pier or breakwater and as the conditions at his chosen fishing spot were much the same as those on his home ground he used the same technique and most effective it was too. First he attracted the mullet by lowering a mesh bag full of bread scraps into the water where the action of the waves kept a constant stream of bait particles drifting away from the bag. This soon brought the shoaling mullet nosing right up to the groundbait bag in search of food. Once this occurred the angler baited his plain leger tackle (fig 76) with bread and lowered it down amongst the hungry fish. The tackle was allowed to sink three or four feet and was then held suspended from the rod tip. To my mind this was a crude way

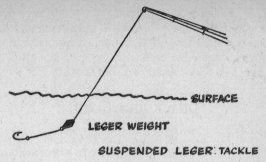

SURFACE

LEGER WEIGHT

SUSPENDED LEGER TACKLE

Fig 76

of taking fish, but it worked well and at the end of the tide the angler concerned went off home with over a dozen fine fish to his credit. Recently, this same method has been used to take a number of big mullet from the breakwater at Dover. The suspended leger can only be used from sheer rocks which fall into deep water, but when these conditions occur it is well worth trying.

# CHAPTER 7

## Pollack and Coalfish

If ever there was an obliging species it is the pollack, that handsome hard-fighting salt water game fish which is second only to the bass when it comes to fighting ability, a fish against which any sporting angler should be proud to pit his skill and tackle. From Land's End to the Scottish islands pollack are plentiful practically wherever rocks and sunken reefs abound, and to the light tackle enthusiast the pollack has a great deal to offer; for where one is found there too will be others, each more than ready to pull down a sea float or snatch greedily at a shiny artificial lure. Because of this the pollack is an ideal quarry for the rock angler, and although inshore pollack rarely reach the weights of their big offshore cousins, they do occasionally weigh as much as 10 lb, although the average weight of inshore fish is generally 2 lb to 4 lb. The record rod-caught pollack was taken in deep water off Newquay on the North Cornish coast. This fine fish weighed 23 lb 8 oz. A 38-pounder was, however, caught on a long line set by a Mevagissey boat somewhere off the South Cornish coast. Many other big pollack have fallen to commercial fishing methods and there can be little doubt that the finest pollack fishing is to be had over the deep offshore marks.

Up until 1967, pollack were regarded by ichthyologists as true members of the cod family. Now the pollack has been reclassified as *Pollachius pollachius*, its nearest relative being the coalfish, *Pollachius virens*. Many anglers are confused by these two fish and commonly mistake one for the other. Both are 'round' fish and both have a distinctive lateral line. The lateral line of the pollack is dark, whereas the lateral line of the coalfish is white. The underjaw of the pollack protrudes well beyond its upper jaw, while that of the coalfish only protrudes slightly. The tail of the coalfish has a pronounced fork while the tail of a true pollack is only slightly forked (fig 77). Adult coalfish have a single barbel dependent from the lower jaw. Pollack lack this appendage. Both species are frequently caught

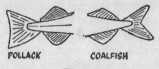

POLLACK          COALFISH

Fig 77

over the same ground, and unless you know what characteristics to look for in the individual species it is very easy to become confused. Both species are common along most of the rocky western coast of Scotland, an area which has great potential. The coasts of Devon, Cornwall, Wales and Western Ireland are excellent places to pollack fish, although it is my belief that the west coast of Scotland will prove to be one of the finest of all pollack and coalfish areas. Several years ago I fished various shore marks from the Kyle of Lochalsh up to Cape Wrath and the average weight of the pollack I caught during this trip was over 6 lb, and I caught a great many during my visit. Practically none of the rock fishing marks along this vast stretch of coastline have been exploited and the deep, clear, food-rich waters are full of big fish. This is truly a shore fisherman's paradise, for with float or artificial baits sport comes fast and furious.

One of my favourite venues was at the mouth of Loch Broom near Ullapool in Wester Ross. This was comfortable fishing from safe rock ledges which dropped directly into deep water, but I found equally good fishing farther north at places like Achiltibuie, Achnacarnin, Badcall Bay, and many others. Between Cape Wrath and Thurso I found many more likely places. Unfortunately, by the time I had reached this area I had to limit my fishing to an hour to two at odd places. I did, however, catch some fine pollack and coalfish during the process but I feel that altogether I only scratched the surface of the fine fishing that is to be had along this magnificent seaboard.

## Feeding Habits

Pollack and coalfish are fast-moving predators which live by preying on small fish of many kinds. Both species show a liking for marine worms and prawns. Practically any small fish can be used as bait, but I found I have caught most of my better fish on sand eels, elvers, and small rock fish, i.e. gobbies, blennies, etc; prawns also make a first-class bait. In Scottish waters I have caught some fine coalfish on limpet. Both species of fish feed in similar ways. Generally speaking, during the daytime both fish are to be found hunting very close to the sea bed; at twilight, however, these fish leave the bottom and rise towards the surface: to take advantage of this it is best to float fish at this time of day, so that the bait can be presented at the correct level. The normal run of medium-sized pollack and coalfish usually arrive in inshore waters during early April and stay until the late autumn, but a run of much larger fish generally occurs during late September. These fish stay until early January, but very few anglers realize this, and in many areas pollack fishermen turn to other species as soon as September arrives.

Rock fishing during the winter months is far from comfortable and very few anglers usually brave the elements. Because of this they miss a lot of good fishing, for the winter run of pollack is comprised of big fish, double-figure specimens being far from uncommon. I have taken several of these while fishing during the winter from marks which during the summer time produce only medium-sized fish, and my angling notes show that the average weight of winter-caught pollack is around 7 lb, several pounds heavier than that of summer-caught fish. I must admit that the bulk of my winter rock fishing has been done along the south Cornish coast, so I can give no opinions of winter pollack or coalfish in other areas. I have received reports that it can be good, providing the angler has the stamina to withstand the bleak winter weather while fishing from exposed rocks.

The angler who wishes to catch larger than average fish during the summer months will be well advised to seek areas which only rarely see other anglers. Years ago when I lived at Mevagissey in south Cornwall I took many fine pollack from the rocks at the foot of the Dodman on Deadman Head. Fishing this spot involved a fearsome climb directly down the vast cliffs. In my opinion it was worth it for the fish I caught were exceptionally large for the time of year; at the same time the climb was a frightening experience and not one that I would recommend to others. I only quote it as an example of finding and exploiting a practically unfished area. Big pollack like most big fish shy away from the more accessible rock fishing marks where most anglers congregate. Peaceful sandy coves surrounded by rocks are a good place to try, but these are best fished during the late evening or early morning before or after the bathers and sun worshippers arrive or leave for the day. During the winter months when these coves are deserted good fishing can be had at midday, providing the tides are right.


*Tackle*

Pollack and coalfish are obliging creatures which will snap up almost any moving bait which comes their way. Because of this and the comparatively small average size of most shore-caught specimens it is possible to fish for both species with comparatively light tackle. I have two pollack or coalfish outfits, one for throwing light artificial baits, the other for float fishing or light bottom fishing. For spinning I use a standard glass carp type rod, and fixed-spool reel loaded with 8 lb bs nylon and for float or bottom fishing I use an SU glass carp rod, which again is coupled with a fixed-spool reel carrying two hundred yards of 12 lb bs line. The stepped-up carp rod will throw comparatively heavy tackle a considerable distance, and as I usually prefer to employ natural baits for large pollack I use this outfit a great deal when fishing isolated areas noted for larger than average pollack. I also use it for winter fishing for the same reason. Pollack and coalfish are big-mouthed ever-hungry fish which usually take and swallow a bait in one gulp. Because of this largish hooks are essential; for livebaits I use a size 3/0 hook and for fish strips, elvers, prawns and worm baits a size 1/0. Even small pollack weighing less than a pound have little difficulty in swallowing a big hook, and a seven-pounder has an enormous mouth, so largish hooks are essential. A selection of split shot, drilled bullets, and barrel leads should also be carried.

## Floats

For general pollack fishing using light baits, small sliding floats of the type used for wrasse fishing should be employed. For livebaiting a more substantial float should be employed otherwise the bait will continually drag the float beneath the surface. Pollack are bold biters, which seldom drop a bait once they

WOODEN PEG

PLASTIC TUBE CAN BE USED IN PLACE OF PEG TO TURN FLOAT INTO SLIDING TYPE

PEG TYPE PIKE FLOAT (FISHING GAZETTE)

Fig 78

have taken it, so any reasonably streamlined float can be used. I use small-sized 'Fishing Gazette type' pike floats when live-baiting for pollack and coalfish. This type of float is supplied with a peg (fig 78) which allows you to fix the float at the re-quired depth. This arrangement is perfectly adequate for fishing in shallow water, but in deep gullies or harbours where the bait may have to be fished at a depth of 20 ft or more a sliding type float must be used. I make this up from 'Fishing Gazette' floats by substituting a suitable length of plastic tube for the wooden peg (fig 78). This is a simple operation which converts a fixed float into a sliding float in a matter of seconds. For daytime fishing an orange-topped float is best, but at twilight when visibility is poor a yellow-topped float is easier to see than any other colour. As with all forms of shore fishing, tackle losses while float fishing are high, so it is advisable to carry at least four floats with you at all times.

## Artificial Baits

Pollack and coalfish fall readily to artificial lures of many kinds, but probably the best of all the lures is the plain rubber eel (fig 79), a bait which has accounted for many fine specimens. Rubber eels can be obtained in a wide range of colours,

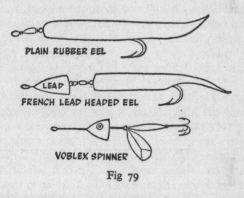

Fig 79

each of which will catch fish on the right day. Why fish will take a green eel one day and a black one the next is inexplicable but to make sure of a fish or two it pays to carry a selection of eels in various colours. In my experience the most killing colours are red or brown, but if the fish are being finicky then a brighter colour may do the trick. Professional fishermen make up their own rubber eels from suitable lengths of soft surgical rubber, but good eels cost only a few pence or so to buy from a tackle shop so unless you like making up your own baits it is best to purchase ready-made eels. When buying rubber eels always make certain they are manufactured from soft rubber, for some commercially made eels have semi-stiff tails which will not wave about as the bait is being retrieved. These baits are of little or no use. A bait with a soft flexible tail, however, is deadly and will catch both pollack and coalfish when all other baits fail to attract the fish.

There is a French-made lure known as a lead-headed eel (fig 79). These baits are manufactured with heads of various weights, and designed for long casting. I use these lures when fishing deepish water, for I find that in shallow water they have to be retrieved far too rapidly to attract fish. A slow retrieve is impossible for the weighted bait sinks to the sea bed and usually gets caught up in some solid underwater obstruction. In deep water the angle of the line between the rod tip and the bait keeps the lure well above the sea bed, even when the bait is being slowly retrieved. I find that most of the fish I catch on this lure hook themselves. This is probably due to the weighted head of the bait, for it doesn't occur very often when a plain rubber eel is used. But spoons of the voblex type (fig 79) are also extremely good pollack and coalfish lures. Originally these baits were designed for use in fresh water. Because of this they should be cleaned carefully after use, otherwise corrosion will quickly ruin the hooks and tarnish the metal bodies of the lures. This is a job which should be done at the end of the day's fishing. Any delay will give the salt time to seriously corrode the metalwork. The best way of cleaning lures is to wash them thoroughly in fresh water to remove the salt then thoroughly wipe each bait over with a rag which is impregnated with a light machine oil. The only other lure which I use for pollack and coalfish is an elongated mackerel type lure

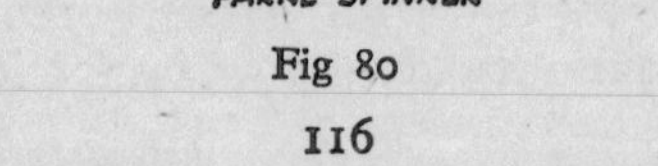

FARNE SPINNER

Fig 80

known as a farne spinner (fig 80). These are simple yet highly effective baits which seem to be most attractive to both pollack and coalfish. The size of artificial baits rather depends on the size of fish normally encountered in a particular area. If, for example, the average weight of fish you expect to catch is between 1 lb and 2 lb then a smallish lure will suffice, but where larger fish are known to exist then a biggish bait should be used. Rubber eels up to 6 in or 7 in in length can be used with confidence, for pollack seem to show a preference for large eels. Occasionally when I require a few small pollack for conger bait I resort to tiny 3 in and 4 in eels which are absolutely deadly for the very small fish I wish to catch. As a rule, half an hour's spinning with one of these tiny eels produces enough bait-sized pollack for a full night's congering. Once, when I accidentally left my artificial lure box at home, I made do with a single hook to which I lashed two or three lengths of red rubber band weighted by a couple of large split shot. This makeshift bait worked beautifully and I soon filled a plastic bag with bait-sized pollack.

*Natural Baits*

Any small live creature is fair game where pollack and coalfish are concerned, consequently the angler who prefers to use a natural bait rather than an artificial lure has plenty of baits to choose from. Strips of squid, mackerel, and herring are the most used baits, but small live fish, prawns, hard- and soft-backed crabs, limpets, mussels and worms are all excellent fish catchers. In Scotland large limpets are the favourite bait. These are only rarely used in the south of England, but I have found them to be quite effective, and nowadays I regard them as a good standby bait which is always available when other baits are unobtainable. Both pollack and coalfish are greedy creatures and I have always found that a large bait catches more fish than a small one. This applies particularly to fish strip baits, which should be cut from the belly of a mackerel or herring in the following fashion. First lay the fish on a bait cutting board, then cut a tapered 5 in strip of bait from the belly or flanks of the fish (fig 81). A razor blade or modelling knife is best, for being sharp and thin they make a neat job. This is important, for the bait should be cut to resemble a sand eel, and a ragged cut spoils this effect.

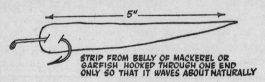

STRIP FROM BELLY OF MACKEREL OR GARFISH HOOKED THROUGH ONE END ONLY SO THAT IT WAVES ABOUT NATURALLY

Fig 81

The fish cutting should be hooked once through the square end so that it is free to waver about freely with the flow of the water. Bunched baits are unattractive and seldom catch decent fish. Few anglers seem to realize the importance of correct bait presentation, but it's no use having large quantities of expensive tackle if your bait is badly presented, for it's the bait not the tackle that catches the fish. Livebaits are of course easy to present properly, for being whole and alive their shape and movements attract predatory fish. Small rock fish are easy to catch from rock pools, and bait-sized blennies can be found in quantity under weed-covered stones during the low water period. Livebaits are easy to keep alive, and providing the water is changed fairly regularly they keep well in a large tin with a perforated lid. If possible this should be sunk in a deep rock pool, or hung in deepish water so that fresh sea water is continually filtering through. For pollack fishing I like to lip-hook my livebaits, and for this I use a 2/0 or 3/0 silvered hook, as I believe the plating on the hook helps to attract fish to the bait. Collecting bait can be great fun and an hour spent turning over rocks and raking in rock pools can produce enough bait for several full days' fishing. One such bait that can usually be collected in large numbers are elvers. These are the young of the freshwater eel and anywhere where there is a trickle of fresh water you will find elvers hiding under flat stones. Catching them is quite an art for being slippery and fast-moving they are difficult to pick up, but once the trick of elver-collecting

118

has been mastered half an hour's work will produce dozens of bait-sized little eels. Elvers are best kept in a box or tin, containing a little damp sand and a few handfuls of fresh wet seaweed. If they are kept in a tin of sea water they die very quickly. Elvers are a wonderful bait for pollack, coalfish and bass. Generally, they are 3 in to 5 in long and very thin so it is best to use a smallish hook when using elvers as bait, a size 1 or 2 being ideal. Elvers are born contortionists and because of this the hook point should be passed directly through the back of the bait, directly behind its head (fig 82). This does them little

ELVER HOOKED JUST
BEHIND HEAD

Fig 82

harm and makes them swim about in a natural fashion. If you try to lip-hook elver baits, they simply screw themselves up into a ball and neatly lever themselves off the hook. A bait hooked through the back is unable to do this. Sand eels (see bass chapter) can of course be lip- or back-hooked without fear of this happening, but elvers are a different proposition. Crabs can be used whole or in halves, prawns should be used alive, either singly or in bunches.

## METHODS

### Spinning

Spinning is a sporting and pleasant way of catching both pollack and coalfish, and is the ideal method for the angler who likes to keep on the move. One of the nice things about spinning is the fact that it allows the angler to cover vast amounts of water during the course of a single day, something which the float or bottom fisherman is unable to do. One of the best places to catch pollack and coalfish on artificial lures is a weed-grown gully between two rocky reefs. In these places the fish spend their time either lurking amongst the thick bottom weed or patrolling along the submerged rock walls just above the weed beds. A spinner or rubber eel worked steadily along just above the weed or close to the rocks will usually produce rapid results. For fishing under these circumstances light baits should be used, and these should be retrieved at a steady speed so that they work at a set level a foot above the beds of seaweed (fig 83). Any break in the rate of retrieve will result in the bait

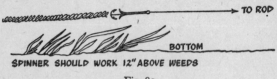

SPINNER SHOULD WORK 12" ABOVE WEEDS

Fig 83

dropping into the weed, where it will probably become snagged up. To add a little extra life to the bait the rod tip can be moved gently from side to side so that the bait zig-zags back through the water, but at no time should the rate of retrieve be slowed down during this process.

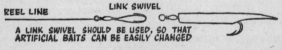

A LINK SWIVEL SHOULD BE USED, SO THAT
ARTIFICIAL BAITS CAN BE EASILY CHANGED

Fig 83A

A dozen casts in any one gully will show whether or not pollack or coalfish are present for they are both active hunters and if the bait isn't taken during these dozen casts, it is fairly safe to assume that no fish are about. If this is the case there is no point in wasting further time, so the angler should move on to the next likely spot in search of fish. Both species are shoal fish and where you catch one you should get more, so if a fish is caught it pays to stay on and work the bait through every fishable inch of the area. In deep water it is possible to vary

the rate of retrieve, so that the bait flutters and vibrates entic-
ingly through the water. Once again the fish will spend most of
their time close to the bottom, so when fishing deeper than
average water larger heavier baits should be used. Obviously
the angler who keeps on the move will find himself fishing a
deep hole one minute and a shallow one the next. Each will
call for a change of lure so to save time it pays to tie a link
swivel (see fig 83A) to the reel line so that baits can be clipped
on and off in a moment. Never tie artificial lures directly to the
reel line, for each type of lure will twist and kink the line to
such an extent that it will soon become unusable. Small dead
fish or sand eels can also be used for the sink and draw style
of fishing. Like spinning this is a roving style of angling which
can be most effective, but the angler must be prepared to lose
a fair amount of terminal tackle if he adopts this style of
angling.

In really weed-choked gullies or amongst sharp rocks it is
impossible to use the sink and draw technique but in areas
which have flat sandy bottoms this can be a deadly method.
To fish a bait in this way, the tackle should be made up leger
fashion, using a $\frac{1}{2}$ oz or $\frac{3}{4}$ oz drilled bullet as a weight. This
should be stopped by a split shot clamped on to the line 12 in
or 18 in from the hook. To bait up, the reel line should be
threaded through the mouth of the dead fish bait, and brought
out at its vent. The hook should then be tied to the end of the
reel line and pulled back so that it protrudes from the bait's
vent. A large swan shot should then be clipped on to the line
as close to the mouth of the bait as possible (fig 84). This will
stop the bait from sliding up the line during casting. To work
the bait properly it should be cast out to the required area and
then allowed to sink to the sea bed. Next the rod tip should
be lifted and at the same time a yard or so of line should be
reeled in. Then the rod tip should be dropped so that the bait
falls back to the sea bed. Being lighter in the water than the
leger weight the bait tends to flutter down in a most attractive
fashion. This process should be repeated until either a fish
takes the bait or a fresh cast is called for. This is a method
which will often catch larger than average fish, and although

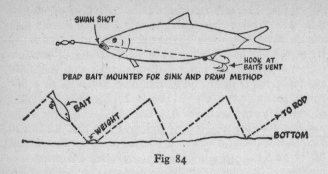

SWAN SHOT

HOOK AT BAITS VENT

DEAD BAIT MOUNTED FOR SINK AND DRAW METHOD

BAIT

WEIGHT

TO ROD

BOTTOM

Fig 84

it is messy compared with true spinning, it is well worth a try, particularly when the larger autumn fish are running inshore. One bait can be used to catch two or three fish, for neither pollack nor coalfish damage a bait much when they strike at it.

## Bottom Fishing

True bottom fishing is seldom practised by pollack fishermen for neither pollack nor coalfish take much notice of static bait, although I have had several good pollack on legered herring or squid baits intended for bass, but as a rule the only legered bait that will catch fish is a live sand eel or rock fish. Nothing special is required in the way of terminal tackle for bottom fishing and a standard bass type leger rig (see bass chapter) will suffice. Very occasionally I have used a paternoster to take pollack; as a static method this is a poor fish catcher but as a moving method of angling it can produce excellent catches. For pollack fishing the plain nylon paternoster which is described in the wrasse chapter is ideal, but the distance between hook trace and lead should be increased to 3 ft or 4 ft, so that the bait works well above the sea bed. This is a technique which works best over a fairly level sea bed. Bait should be a strip of squid or mackerel cut to the shape of a sand eel. Basically this tackle is worked in the same way as the sink and draw technique already described, the tackle being bounced back in a series of jumps that lifts the bait and lead well off the sea bed. This odd movement seems to fascinate both pollack and coalfish and in Cornwall and Scotland I have used this method to take some fine big fish. When very big fish are known to be in the area the usual single hook can be changed to a size 4 treble hook to which three suitable bait strips are attached (fig 85). Each bait strip flutters and wiggles as the

THREE FISH STRIPS ON TREBLE HOOK

Fig 85

tackle is being retrieved and this movement seems to be irresistible to the larger fish. Quite apart from pollack and coalfish other species come to this triple bait, and I once caught a bass from a mark near Mevagissey on this bait which tipped the scales at $11\frac{1}{4}$ lb, a grand fish which came as a totally unexpected bonus. Many large fish tend to become scavengers but not so the pollack and coalfish, which prefer a lively moving bait to a static one at any time.

## The Driftline

For fishing from rock ledges or harbour walls which drop directly into deep water, it is possible to dispense with floats or weights and to fish the bait as naturally as possible. This is known as driftlining and is a technique which is best used in fairly rough water where the bait will be swirled about by the action of the sea. Under these conditions the driftline can be a deadly method. Large fish cuttings, live or dead sand eels or small fish can all be used as baits for driftline fishing. To help keep the bait circulating the reel line should be thoroughly smeared with a good line flotant. This will keep most of the line floating on the surface where it will help to support the bait. The floating line can also be used as a bite indicator, for when a fish takes the bait the floating line will straighten out or shoot off across the surface, a sure sign that a fish has taken the bait and bolted with it. Pollack and coalfish seldom drop a bait once they have decided to take it, consequently a fast strike is seldom required. Usually it is only necessary to tighten the line to set the hook.

In really rough water a bubble float can be used to support the bait (fig 86). This is not true driftline fishing but it can

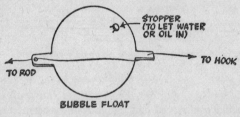

Fig 86

be effective when rough seas make it difficult to fish. Bubble floats are bulky at the best of times and only the smallest sized bubble floats should be used. These floats are constructed so that they can be partially filled with water. This adds weight for casting purposes. I substitute oil for water and seal the removable stopper over with clear glue. Oil doesn't evaporate and the float can be permanently weighted ready for use at all times. One disadvantage of the bubble float is the fact that the float is of a fixed type, therefore it has to be set so that it can be easily cast out. This means that one is restricted to fishing at 8 ft or 10 ft. This is no problem in shallow water but in very deep water it makes it impossible to fish properly. Used in the right places, however, a bubble float can be a valuable piece of equipment.

*General Float Fishing*

Of all the many methods that can be used to catch pollack and coalfish I like float fishing the best, for both species are bold biters, which thump a float down with a savage pull. This makes for exciting fishing and as float tackle covers a lot of water this method can be used to thoroughly search through a likely area or gully. In Scotland where the rocks fall steeply away into very deep water, I often fished at a depth of thirty or more feet. Under these conditions I found that float tackle was by far the best type of terminal gear to use and I caught a great many large pollack and coalfish on it. In water as deep as this I used a fairly large sliding float. When I say large, I mean by my standards, and not by the standards of the people who manufacture most of the sea floats that find their way into tackle shops. These commercially made floats seem to be designed on a gigantic scale and are far too large and cumbersome to be of any practical use, except as shark floats. If a sea float requires more than $\frac{1}{2}$ oz or $\frac{3}{4}$ oz to cock it, then in my opinion it is too large for general fishing. There are of course some useful patterns available, but it pays to be choosy when selecting sea floats.

In shallow gullies of the type that abound along the Devon and Cornish coastlines a fixed float can be used, but where the water is deeper than the length of the rod a sliding float should be employed. Float fishing for pollack and coalfish is a simple method, and providing the float is set so that the bait is suspended a foot or so above the sea bed fish should be caught. I said earlier that pollack and to a lesser extent coalfish alter their feeding levels at different times of the day. This means basically that during the brightest part of the day these fish spend most of their time hunting or lurking close to the sea bed. As the light fades, however, the fish rise to the surface and feed just under the waves. The evening angler then should adjust his tackle accordingly, otherwise his bait will hang below the feeding level. In inshore waters late evening and night sessions are best, for it is at this time that the largest fish begin to prowl around. Providing the tide is right and the rocks are safe to fish from, night fishing can provide excellent sport. It is of course impossible to watch a float after dark, but a float should still be used to support the bait at the required depth. This is the true function of a float, and the fact that it can also be used as a bite indicator is of secondary importance. At night the line between rod tip and float should be kept taut so that although the float cannot be seen a bite can be felt through the rod tip. This is the technique I use for float fishing at night. Besides pollack and coalfish I have caught bass, dory, red bream and several other species as well by using this technique.

## Sunken Float Tackle

This is an interesting style of fishing which is a cross between float and paternoster tackle. Originally this gear was devised for pier fishing, the idea being to keep the bait up off the sea bed so that the bait was kept up out of reach of the crabs. I adapted it for rock fishing, where it proved to be particularly successful. I use this tackle for fishing over a reef (fig 87) where normal tackle would quickly become snagged on the top

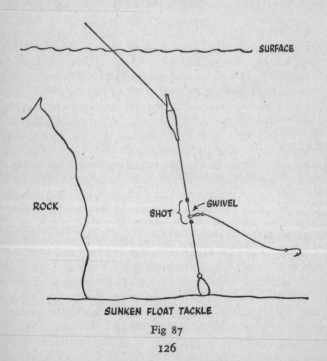

SURFACE

ROCK

SHOT { SWIVEL

SUNKEN FLOAT TACKLE

Fig 87

of the submerged rocks. With the sunken float tackle this doesn't occur very often, for providing the rod is held high so that the line between the rod tip and submerged float is taut, the angle between the two will keep the reel line from becoming hung up. The tackle is set up paternoster style with the float set so that it is sunk two or three feet below the surface. A smallish float and a large lead are essential if this unusual tackle is to function correctly. Bites are felt through the rod tip as in normal paternoster fishing. Although this particular method is limited, it can be used to fish ground which would be impossible to cover with more conventional tackle. Because of this it is a useful standby style and well worth remembering. It is rare to become snagged when retrieving this type of tackle for the float seems to lift the lead up and over any obstructions.

# CHAPTER 8

# Tope, Dogfish and Sharks

*Tope*

Tope have often been called the 'poor man's shark', a name which I think suits them admirably, for these big hard-fighting fish offer the average shore angler the opportunity to catch a really large fish without too much capital outlay. The tope is a typical member of the shark family, having two dorsal fins and the usual prominent gill slits. The general coloration is grey or greyish-brown and the underparts are white. Tope up to 7 ft in length have been caught by commercial fishing methods, and fish up to nearly 75 lb in weight have been taken on rod and line.

Nowadays most tope anglers go afloat in search of their favourite quarry, their argument being that the larger fish usually fall to the boat anglers. This is undoubtedly true but many very big tope can also be caught from the shore, although shore fishing is a much slower form of angling. At the same time it is much more exciting, for a big tope hooked in fairly shallow water can put up a spectacular fight. The first tope I ever hooked from the shore leaped clean out of the water when it felt the hook, and then took off like a scalded cat in the general direction of France. It was only the fact that I was using a large reel carrying nearly three hundred yards of 20 lb bs line that saved the day, for with two hundred yards of line trailing astern the fish was still going strongly. The drag of the line through the water and the strain imposed by my well-bent rod slowed the fish up before it went much farther and its next run was much shorter. This fish weighed 49 lb, and twenty minutes after it was beached I was into another, which after a very similar battle tipped the scales at 45 lb. Both fish were females, and on only one occasion have I ever taken a male tope while shore fishing. During my commercial fishing career I took a great many tope on rod and line from deep offshore marks, and in the deep water I found the bulk of my catches consisted of male tope weighing between 25 lb and 35 lb. Other tope anglers have confirmed that they catch more female tope in shallow water than male fish, and vice versa. Moreover, many of the females have either been full of young when landed or have given birth on the beach, so that it could be that the pregnant females come inshore to drop their young, leaving most of the smaller male fish to feed out in the deep water grounds. It is interesting to note that when captured females have shed their young on the shore I have always made a point of putting the little fish back into the sea where they have usually swum off apparently none the worse for their unusual experience.

Tope have a wide distribution and are common round most parts of the British Isles. The Irish coasts provide first-class tope fishing, and at many places on the Irish, Welsh, English and Scottish coastlines it is possible to shore fish for tope. In Scotland where sea fishing is still in its infancy, I once saw a pack of big tope scavenging about in the clear waters near the ferry that runs from the mainland to the Isle of Skye. This pack held some very big fish which continually broke the surface of the water close to the rocks on which I stood. The only other place I have seen tope do this is at Park Shore in the Solent, where on warm still evenings it is sometimes possible to watch two or three very big tope working quietly along a few yards out from the beach. To the best of my knowledge very few tope have ever been caught from Scottish marks, probably because until recently no one bothered much with sea angling there, and as yet only a handful of places have ever been properly fished, and these have never been fished for tope, so the possibilities of the Scottish shore marks are totally unknown as far as tope fishing is concerned although the potential is enormous. Cornwall is also an area which could easily provide first-class shore fishing for tope, but once again there is little interest among local anglers who prefer to fish for bass, pollack or conger. Consequently very little is known about the movement of tope in Cornish waters. Although I have never done a lot of serious tope fishing from Cornish shore marks I have caught a few tope from both the south and north sides of the peninsula and my experiences have shown that tope are more prolific in these waters than is generally supposed.

## Conservation – For and Against

Tope, like so many large predatory fish, have a bad reputation with anglers and commercial fishermen alike, the theory being that the big fish eat the small fish and spoil the fishing for the rod-and-line and commercial men. They are also accused of tearing nets. Because of this belief practically every tope that is caught is killed and either dumped back into the sea or taken home and buried in the garden to fertilize the rose bushes. Few people look at the problem logically and most just follow the crowd. To some extent this is understandable for a tope is a big fish which lives by preying on smaller fish, but whether or not the amount of little fish consumed by tope or, for that matter, other predators, has any marked effect on the fish population in a given area is extremely doubtful. One inshore trawler probably does more damage to immature fish in a single week than a tope does in its whole lifetime, and a good many anglers who should know better are consistently guilty of killing far too many small fish without giving any thought to future sport. A visit to practically any hard-fished area will usually disclose pathetic heaps of tiny pollack, flatfish, bream, wrasse, etc, which are left to die slowly well above the tide line, food only for the gulls or harbour cats, yet the very anglers who leave those heaps of immature fish are usually the first to complain and blame tope or other predators when a once good fishing mark ceases to provide sport. All predators are in my opinion essential, for by killing sick or injured fish, and by keeping the small fish in check they help to keep the balance of nature. If there were no predators then the sea would be packed with tiny stunted fish, fish unable to grow to a respectable size because their natural food supplies would be exhausted. To stop this occurring nature has provided predators, and the tope is one that in my opinion does a good job. I have killed some tope, but only the odd very large specimens which I required for photographic purposes; the rest of the tope I have caught have been, where possible, returned alive and I hope unharmed to the sea; because of this I seldom gaff the fish I catch, preferring where possible to tail them so that they suffer no bodily damage. This is difficult to do when fishing from high rocks, but whenever possible I tail a fish. If you happen to hook a real monster, then use the gaff. Big fish are very near to the end of their life span and rather than take the chance of losing a potential record-breaker, it is far better to use the gaff and make certain of the fish. A dead tope is at best a smelly, awkward object, and although some people eat tope steaks, they are an acquired taste, and my advice to all tope fishermen is to return the majority of the fish they can catch to the water.

## Time of Year

Tope normally appear in inshore waters during May and stay to the end of September. Their arrival depends much on water temperature; if, for example, the weather in April and May is warm, then the fish will arrive early on in the month. If, on the other hand, the weather is cold and blustery, then the fish will not appear until the end of the month. I once caught several tope while shore fishing in Cornwall during mid-October. The weather then was exceptionally good, and this no doubt had encouraged the fish to linger on a little later than usual. During June there is often a rush of tope into inshore waters. This lasts two or three weeks, then another inshore rush starts at the end of August. At these times sport can be fast and furious; in between times one has to be content with the odd fish or two.

Tope are predatory fish which live by preying on small fish of many kinds. In some areas pouting form the mainstay of their diet while in other places small flatfish or mackerel seem to be their main quarry. Tope will also eat worms, shore crabs, hermit crabs and cuttle fish. In the Solent waters one often finds dead cuttle fish with their heads and tentacles missing. This is a sure sign that the tope packs are on the move. I have seen several tope caught on crab and worm baits, meant for bass, and in Cornwall quite a few good tope have been taken on legered sand eels. On several occasions when I have caught tope, I have found that the small green shore crabs which have been systematically destroying my baits have suddenly ceased operations shortly after I have had a tope bite, proving to my mind that the crabs have learned to take cover when there is a tope about. I have never tried using crabs as tope bait, but several tope which I have landed have regurgitated quantities of small crabs, so it would seem that tope are not averse to making a meal of crabs.

All the tope I have caught while shore fishing have been taken during the daytime, or during the evening; so far I have yet to take a tope at night from shallow water although I have caught several good-sized tope while night fishing from boats anchored in deep water. Whether it would be possible to consistently catch tope from the shore at night no one as yet knows and to prove whether or not it would be possible would take up a considerable amount of time, time which no one seems to be prepared to spend on a possibily fruitless project. Personally, I believe that an intensive night fishing campaign could produce excellent results, for in areas where tope are caught by daytime shore fishermen, many night anglers regularly report being smashed up by large fast-moving fish of unidentified species. I have spoken to a number of anglers who have been broken up in this fashion and their descriptions of the bite and fight of the fish suggest to me that in most cases tope are the culprits. Proving it is a different matter, and until a number of these 'unknown' fish have been beached it will be impossible to draw any definite conclusions as to the true identity of these tackle breakers.

## Effect of Weather on Tope Movement

Tope are much affected by climatic conditions, and unless the weather is right the chances of catching tope while rock or shore fishing are slight. Hot, sultry weather is best, particularly if there is little or no wind to ruffle the surface of the sea. In these conditions, tope will come right inshore to forage in really shallow water and on several occasions when these conditions have prevailed I have watched tope wallow long right on the surface, often in water which is barely deep enough to cover their bodies. Even under ideal conditions, however, tope will only behave in this way if they believe themselves to be safe from danger. To avoid disturbing the fish, the sensible angler will refrain from violent movement, and where possible will keep well below the skyline: unless these precautions are strictly observed the tope will quickly take alarm and disappear out to sea.

I have caught good tope on cold, wet, windy days but prefer when possible to fish on warm, windless days. Tope fishing is at best a very chancy sport, for these fish are nomadic wanderers which seldom stay in any one locality for any length of time. Consequently you are fishing in the hope that one or more of these fish will decide to wander through the area in search of food. Very often the angler can spend a series of blank days waiting for a bite, yet when the fish do come, sport is often fast and furious, and on more than one occasion while using two rods I have had two fish on at one time. Normally this results in a lost set of terminal tackle, but once I was fortunate enough to land both fish one after the other: one of these weighed 37 lb and the other 42 lb. Half an hour later I got another 40-pounder. These fish were all caught during an evening session, and came at the end of a week during which I had fished daily with no results whatsoever.

Fresh baits are essential for tope fishing, and where possible I like to catch my bait to order. Pout whiting are my normal baits, for these greedy little fish are usually easy to catch and are very attractive to hungry tope. Mackerel fillets or whole 'joey' mackerel are another good bait, but they must be freshly caught. A 'joey' is a very small mackerel about 8 in long. These little fish often occur in vast shoals and are easy to catch on spinners or feathers. Commercial fishermen will often save you a few of these little fish for bait, and at the cost of an occasional pint in the local a regular supply of fresh bait can usually be arranged. I once fished from a series of rocks surrounded by sandy ground. Here I found that frozen flatfish fillets worked as well as other baits. Frozen herring fillets were also good, although nowadays the suppliers don't seem to be marketing herring fillets any more. On ground which is devoid of snags and weed, live pout whiting are the ideal bait. These should be hooked through the root of the tail. A bait hooked in this fashion is easier to cast than a lip-hooked bait, and it also seems to stay alive longer and work better than a livebait hooked in the mouth. Livebaiting is without doubt a cruel sport, but nature is cruel and by presenting a bait as naturally as possible you will stand more chance of catching fish than the angler who just chucks out a lump of dead fish in the mistaken belief that tope will eat any old rubbish they manage to find. If you are totally against the idea of using a livebait, then by all means use deadbaits and fish fillets, but make sure they are fresh and look as natural as possible. With a whole deadbait it is easy to make it look natural but with fillet baits it is best to tie them firmly to the hook shank and eye (fig 88) so that they fish properly. Nothing looks worse than a tope bait which hangs in a soggy bundle from the end of the hook (fig 88, left) and although it takes a minute or two to lash a bait firmly to the hook shank, it is time well spent, for only bait-robbing scavengers like dogfish and small conger will be attracted to a badly presented fish fillet bait. Darning wool should be used to lash the bait on, colour being immaterial (fig 88, right).

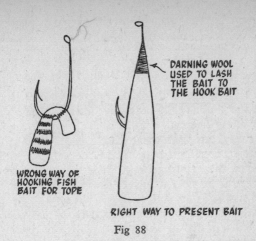

DARNING WOOL
USED TO LASH
THE BAIT TO
THE HOOK BAIT

WRONG WAY OF
HOOKING FISH
BAIT FOR TOPE

RIGHT WAY TO PRESENT BAIT

Fig 88

## TACKLE

*Rods*

A good quality 11 ft or 12 ft long hollow glass beach-caster is the ideal rod for shore tope fishing. There are now many patterns of rod available, and the final choice is left to the individual angler. Most beach-casting rods are designed to cast certain weights; for tope fishing a rod capable of throwing 6 oz to 8 oz leads is about right.

*Reels*

The only kind of reel which is really suitable for shore tope fishing is the multiplier. Fixed-spool reels are simpler to use, but in my opinion don't lend themselves to tope fishing. For one thing, the line capacity of this type of reel is far less than that of a medium-sized multiplier, and the bale arm of a fixed spool soon distorts under the pressure of playing a big hard-fighting fish. My own reel is a Pflueger Sea King, a wide-drummed reel made for long casting and with a good line capacity. The British-made Intrepid Sea Streak is another reel which would be ideal for tope fishing.

## Lines

Providing your reel will hold 250 to 300 yards of line, there is no point in using extra-heavy line. My own choice is a plain monofilament line with a 22 lb bs. This makes long smooth casting easy, cuts down water resistance, and although I have occasionally been broken up, I find I can land most of the tope I hook on this breaking strain. Most breakages occur when anglers refuse to yield an inch of line to a running fish. These tactics may well work with small fish, but not with tope, which should be allowed to run against steady rod pressure. A big tope hooked in shallow water thinks nothing of running out a hundred yards or more of line. Seldom will it take more than this, so providing your reel is capable of holding plenty of line, playing the fish presents little problem. Tope will usually begin to slow up and turn long before the reel line is exhausted, so in my experience I would say it is better to fish with ample light line than to try for tope with an insufficient quantity of strong line. Many beginners, however, believe that brute strength and strong tackle should be sufficient to stop even the largest of fish; this unfortunately is far from the truth and more than once I have seen anglers who have crammed a hundred yards of 40 lb bs line on their reels lose fish which have run out all their line in the first dash and simply carried on going.

## Terminal Tackle

Tope are basically bottom feeders and the most suitable and practical terminal tackle to use for tope fishing is a plain running leger. Tope have sharp teeth and rough skins, both of which can cut through a plain nylon trace. To overcome this the trace should be made from 50 lb or 60 lb bs nylon-covered wire. The ideal tope trace should be 5 ft to 6 ft in length, so that at no time can the skin of the tope come into direct contact with the reel line. I make up my own traces at home, each being made in two sections joined in the middle by a size 2/0 swivel (fig 89), a second swivel of similar size being attached

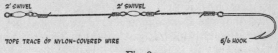

TOPE TRACE OF NYLON-COVERED WIRE                    5/6 HOOK

Fig 89

to the free end of the trace, so that the reel line can be knotted securely to the trace without danger of the knots slipping under pressure. The size of hook depends entirely on the size of the bait. Small whole fish or fillet baits can be mounted on a size 5/0 hook, and large whole fish on size 8/0 or 10/0 hooks. There are many hook patterns available, but my favourite big fish hooks are ring-eyed, forged 'O'Shaughnessy' hooks made by Mustads. These are exceptionally strong and can easily be honed to a sharp point by means of a carborundum stone. The shape of the leger weight is a matter of personal choice, but where distance casting is essential, then bomb- or torpedo-shaped leads should be used (fig 90). The amount of weight

ELONGATED BOMB
WEIGHT FOR CASTING

Fig 90

used depends on prevailing conditions, but wherever possible it pays to keep the weight as small as possible, for there is no point in using an 8 oz lead when a 4 oz one will suffice.

*Sundry Items*

I always carry a supply of extra hooks, swivels and nylon-covered wire, so that if I lose tackle I can always make up a few more traces from stock. A disgorger of the heavy pike type can be useful (fig 91) for tope have tough mouths and removing a hook from a lively fish which you wish to return alive to the water can often be a tricky operation, so for lightly set hooks the long disgorger is ideal. If the fish is deep hooked, then it is best to cut the trace as close to the eye of the hook as possible and release the fish with the hook still in it. This may sound cruel but in practice it is better than cutting the hook out, leaving a raw gaping wound in the process. A small pair of snips is the most useful tool to use for cutting cleanly through a wire trace.

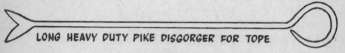

LONG HEAVY DUTY PIKE DISGORGER FOR TOPE

Fig 91

## Tope Fishing Technique

Tope fishing is at best a waiting game, and the keen tope man must be prepared to spend many inactive hours waiting for the first indication that a tope is interested in the bait. Tope are bottom feeders, and as all shore anglers know, a bait legered right on the sea bed attracts the attention of many unwanted creatures which will worry the bait down to nothing in a remarkably short time. Because of this, it pays to check the condition of the bait every thirty minutes or so if the crabs and other scavengers are active and every hour if they are not. Tope are very fussy feeders, and will seldom show any interest in a bait if it is mangled by crab or other vermin.

The distance which the bait should be cast depends on the mark being fished. At some stations where the beach falls directly into deepish water a cast of 25 to 30 yards will be quite sufficient. At others where the water is shallow the bait may have to be cast 60 to 80 yards to reach the fish. If a hole or gully can be located within casting range, it is a good idea to try and drop the bait directly into it, for tope seem to frequent these depressions in the sea bed. Personally, I don't like to hold the rod while tope fishing, for I am sure that tope can feel the slightest vibration of the line and on more than one occasion when I have tried holding the rod I have felt fish pick up the bait and then eject it — something which rarely occurs when the rod is on a rest. Despite their size, strength and speed tope often take a bait gently and very often the first indication of a bite is a gentle 'twitching' of the rod tip. When this occurs the rod should be picked up and lowered to give the fish a little loose line (fig 92). This will usually encourage it to

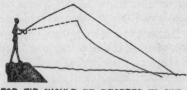

ROD TIP SHOULD BE DROPPED TO GIVE
A BITING TOPE SLACK LINE (DOTTED
LINE INDICATES LOWERED ROD)

Fig 92

run with the bait whereupon a firm strike should set the hook. Under no circumstances should a tope rod be left unattended, nor should the reel be left in the locked position, otherwise the rod will probably rise into the air and disappear for ever out to sea. Once a tope is hooked it should be played firmly out. Never try to bully a big tope or try to bring it to the shore until it is thoroughly played out, otherwise a breakage will almost certainly occur. A lively tope on a short line is usually a lost fish, so take your time, be firm, and make sure your fish is exhausted before you try to gaff or tail it. As I said earlier, it is a shame to kill tope unless you can use them and for this reason I seldom use a gaff although I invariably carry one. If a gaff has to be used to hoist the fish on to the shore, then make sure you drive the gaff right into the soft underparts of the fish and get it ashore as quickly as possible. Tope blood smells terrible so if you intend to carry your catch home, first kill it, then cut its throat and hang its head down over the rocks so that most of its blood drains out. In the case of an extra-large specimen, or possible record-breaker, don't do this until after the fish has been properly weighed in front of witnesses, for loss of blood means loss of weight and in the case of record-breakers every ounce counts.

## Rock Fishing for Shark

There are four common species of shark to be found in the seas around the British Isles. These are: the blue, mako, porbeagle and thresher sharks. Other species do occur occasionally but are so rare that they are of no interest to the sport fisherman. In the west of England, shark fishing has long been recognized as a sporting pastime, and from Torquay down to Penzance and at several places on the north Cornish coast boats specializing in shark fishing are easily obtainable, and any angler wishing to go out for a day's fishing will have little trouble in booking a seat on an organized trip. Most shark boats specialize in catching blue shark; and few porbeagle, thresher or mako sharks are taken in comparison to the large numbers of blue shark which are caught each year. As a rule, most shark boats fish at a distance of at least eleven to twelve miles out from the land, which is probably one reason why they seldom make contact with porbeagle and thresher sharks, both of which undoubtedly spend much of their time in inshore waters where they feed on rock fish, and flatfish of various types.

Shore fishing for shark is a very new sport and so far only one man has met with any great success at this game. This is Jack Shine, whose catches of porbeagle shark have created great interest during the past few years. Mr Shine fishes a rock mark called Green Island which is situated at the entrance to Kiscannon Bay near the town of Lahinch on the west coast of Ireland. I was at Green Island several seasons ago and even at low water it is possible to cast a bait out into five or six fathoms of water, and a boat expedition showed that the sea bed fell away to over fifteen fathoms less than a quarter of a mile from the rocks. Incidentally, Green Island only becomes a true island at the top of the tide when the rocks on the inshore side become fully covered by water. General bottom fishing is very good at this station and no doubt the deep water and plentiful supply of food are the main reason why porbeagle shark frequent the area. Many of the sharks caught by Mr Shine have weighed well over 100 lb, very big fish indeed to tackle from a shore mark, but what a thrill it must be to take one of these giants. From talking to local anglers it seems as though the first porbeagle arrive at Green Island at the end of May or in early June. Where I live on the Hampshire coast, porbeagle don't normally arrive until July, but they do show up in West Country waters at about the same time they arrive off the west coast of Ireland so anyone who intends to try West Country or Irish shore fishing for shark could begin operations during early June.

As I have said, shore fishing for shark is a completely new sport, and in England there are very few spots that I have ever fished which would lend themselves to this form of fishing. One which I have tried, however, is a mark in St Austell Bay (South Cornwall) known as the Black Head. This falls into comparatively deep water and is much favoured by local anglers as a place to catch mackerel. Moreover, big unidentified fish occasionally put in an appearance here and signify their presence by rolling on the surface, or by snatching at hooked fish. No one to my knowledge has ever succeeded in landing one of these unknown fish, although quite a few anglers have had light mackerel tackle broken by them. On the few occasions I have fished the Black Head grounds I have failed to get a bite on my heavy float tackle and large mackerel-baited hooks, but shore fishing for shark is a very chancy occupation and from accounts I have read of Mr Shine's fishing one must be prepared for a great many blank days.

*Other Likely Venues*

Since shore fishing for shark is as yet in its infancy, very little is known of shark movement in inshore waters and anyone wishing to experiment with this type of fishing will be forced to start from scratch and locate his own fishing grounds. So far, only porbeagle shark have been taken in this way, but thresher shark also come in close to the land in search of food and it may prove possible to catch these fish as well. Blue and mako shark are a different proposition entirely and both seem to prefer to keep well offshore, although the mako is a nomadic fish, and it is possible that the odd smallish specimen might occasionally wander into shallowish water.

There are probably a number of places off the Irish coasts which could be tried for shark. In this country, however, likely grounds are more limited although south and north Cornwall have many rock fishing marks which could be worth trying. Pembrokeshire is another possible venue, for at several places along the Pembrokeshire coast the rocks fall into comparatively deep water, and as porbeagle shark are sometimes caught by anglers boat fishing off this coastline it is possible that rock fishing could prove to be a productive proposition. Porbeagle sharks are also fairly common in Scottish waters, and although no one seems to know for certain how prolific they are in northern seas the rock fishing potential of Scotland is well worth investigating, for all round the islands and the west coast proper the rocks drop away into very deep water, and mackerel – which are a favourite food of the porbeagle – are common all around the Scottish coasts, and can often be caught within a few feet of the rocks themselves.

## Tackle

Porbeagle are heavy powerful fish and although I have yet to hook one while shore fishing I have had a few while boat fishing and can vouch for their great fighting ability. In my opinion, a porbeagle fights far harder than a blue shark of similar weight, and despite its short stumpy appearance a porbeagle is a fast-moving fish, capable of bursts of great speed when hooked. Because of this the angler who wishes to try to catch porbeagle from the shore will be well advised to choose his tackle very carefully, paying strict attention to the size of the reel spool, which should be large enough to hold at least

300 yards of 30 lb bs line. At the same time it must be remembered that the bait will have to be cast out well clear of the rocks which means that not only must the reel have a high line capacity but also that it must be of an easily handleable size. Mr Shine, the Green Island expert, uses an Australian side-cast reel, which is probably the best obtainable reel to use, simply because it has a large drum which can easily hold plenty of line, and yet it is designed so that it will cast a bait a long distance with the minimum of effort or over-runs. The Australians use these reels for all forms of fishing, but for everyday work they tend to twist the line far too much for my liking; for sharking, however, where casting is cut to the minimum, they are ideal.

Multiplying reels can also be used, but a reel of this type capable of holding large quantities of heavy line tends to be far too cumbersome for casting work, and for those who can afford it, my advice would be to buy a suitable-sized side-cast reel and use it only for sharking. The rod naturally has to be powerful enough to throw a heavy bait, and strong enough to subdue a fish which may weigh anything up to 200 lb or more in weight. A 10 ft heavy beach-caster in hollow or solid glass is best for this game, although a longer rod can be used if preferred. The terminal tackle should consist of a 6 ft or 7 ft long cable-laid wire trace with a box swivel at one end and a size 8/0 or 10/0 hook at the other. Longer traces would be better but with a 10 ft rod a trace longer than 7 ft would be impossible to cast. Porbeagle, like all shark, have a very rough skin and once this touches the reel line it doesn't take long to rub right through the nylon. Fortunately the average porbeagle is about 5 ft long, so with a 7 ft trace, one has a sporting chance of bringing the fish to the gaff before it has a chance to use the abrasive qualities of its skin on the line itself. While boat fishing I have lost several porbeagle due to the fish rolling the trace round their body, then chaffing through the reel line. This can no doubt occur while rock fishing and fish lost in this fashion must be regarded as part of the game. My own experiences while boat fishing lead me to believe that porbeagle are rather shy fish which will often drop a bait which is suspended beneath a bulky float. Because of this, I like to use the smallest practical floats I can for porbeagle fishing, and although my findings have been made while boat fishing I feel they would almost certainly apply to rock fishing as well. My own shark floats are made from polystyrene (fig 93) but for rock work a

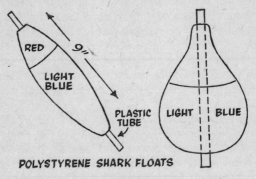

POLYSTYRENE SHARK FLOATS

Fig 93

standard large sea float could be used to good effect. In shallow water porbeagle tend to feed close to the surface and a stop should be tied to the reel line 10 ft or 12 ft from the hook. The sliding float makes casting fairly simple, and when I fished at the Black Head I was able to throw half a mackerel bait 40 or more yards out to sea. I believe Mr Shine uses a rubby-dubby bag containing mashed-up mackerel to attract the fish to within casting range. This is a good idea, and a mesh bag full of mackerel will soon lay a considerable slick of fish oil round a rock mark.

### The Possibilities of Spinning

As a commercial fisherman, I soon discovered that porbeagle will take artificial lures, and I have lost more than one set of mackerel feathers to these marauders, and on one occasion I hooked a biggish porbeagle on a spinner. The light tackle I was using on this occasion snapped within a few moments of the shark taking the lure, but not before I got a good look at the fish. I know anglers fishing for pollack and mackerel at Green Island have had similar experiences so it would seem as though porbeagle are susceptible to artificial lures, and a big spoon or plug bait worked on heavy tackle could easily bring results. This is purely supposition, which I hope to put into operation at the first opportunity. Any angler who has access to a lively rock mark which could produce porbeagle shark could also try artificial baits, for there can be little doubt that a hungry porbeagle will snap at any moving fish-like object.

## Controlling Hooked Fish

If rock-caught porbeagle are anything like boat-caught specimens the angler concerned must be prepared for a hectic and often prolonged struggle during which the fish must be allowed to run. Any real attempt to turn a running porbeagle will probably result in a smashed line, for these fish are fast and strong and you may need every inch of 200 or 300 yards of line before a hooked porbeagle slows up. Once a fish is played out it can be fairly easily gaffed, although here I speak from a boat fishing point of view, and I can well imagine the problems of gaffing a big shark from high rocks. I believe Jack Shine uses a large gaff attached to a series of stout bamboo rods of the type used for unblocking drains. These rods screw into each other and make a strong flexible handle, which when broken down is easily portable. I suggest that you always fish with a companion and use two gaffs to make sure of your fish.

## Final Comments

Rock fishing for shark is in its infancy and no one can really estimate the possibilities of this kind of fishing. So far, to the best of my knowledge only porbeagle have been caught, but thresher shark also work the inshore grounds and where the rocks give way to a flat sandy or gravelly bottom a big fish bait presented on heavy leger tackle could produce the odd thresher. The whole prospect is exciting to say the least and I hope that future seasons will bring more anglers to this sport and with luck some fine fish may be caught.

## Dogfish

Several species of dogfish can be caught by shore fishermen, although very few anglers fish deliberately for them. Generally speaking, most anglers regard all members of the dogfish family as bait-robbing scavengers which make a nuisance of themselves by swallowing baits intended for more worthwhile species. Most rod-caught dogfish are on the small side but one variety, the greater spotted dogfish, or bull huss, grows to a weight of at least 20 lb. Fish of this size are uncommon in shallow water but specimens up to 12 lb or 14 lb in weight are frequently landed. Unlike the other types of dogfish, the bull huss is a strong fish which usually puts up a good fight when hooked. Bull huss, like most types of dogfish, will eat almost any edible matter they come across and unlike most fish they don't seem to differentiate between fresh or stale baits: I have had a good many big bull huss on strips of really stinking mackerel or herring.

During the time I was lobster fishing on a professional scale, I used to find anything up to a dozen or more really big bull huss in my pots each day. How the fish managed to wriggle through the mouth of the pot defeats me, for more often than not it would be necessary to kill the fish and cut it into sections to get it out of the pot. Other fish would get wedged head down in the mouth of the pot, and come to the surface frantically lashing their long bodies about. Many of the bull huss I caught in this way would have broken the rod-caught record quite easily. The fact that they will enter a lobster pot to get at the bait it contains proves that these fish will happily eat stale food, for the chunks of gurnard I used to bait my fleets of pots were invariably half rotten. Bull huss can be caught practically anywhere around the British Isles, particularly in rocky areas. Because of this any rock formation which drops into deepish water is a likely place to try for a big bull huss. In Cornwall where huss are very common I have caught four or five big ones on a single tide, one of my favourite places to fish being Chapel Point, a headland situated near Mevagissey on the south Cornish coast. There are many good fishing positions around this point and at several spots it is easy to cast the bait out into comparatively deep water. Nothing special is required to catch bull huss, just a strong beach-caster, and single-hook paternoster. I use this to keep the bait up off the sea bed away from the small congers and shore crabs. Bait is invariably a generous helping of mackerel or herring strip, although at a pinch almost any type of fish can be used as bait. Bull huss, like all dogfish, appear to be stupid insensitive creatures which will worry a bait down to nothing.

The usual indication of a bite is a series of sharp tugs on the rod tip, and when this occurs the rod tip should be dropped slightly to give the fish a little slack line. This is normally enough to encourage it to take the bait properly. When this happens the huss will begin to move off, swallowing the bait and hook as it goes. A true strike is seldom necessary for the fish will set the hook as it drags at the rod tip. Huss are greedy fish which swallow a bait very quickly and because of this most of the fish you catch will be deeply hooked. Retrieving the hook from a lively huss can be a tricky business for huss have sharp teeth and strong jaws. Their skin is also extremely rough, and they have an unpleasant habit of curling themselves round your arm or hand and then slowly unwinding. This is nasty, for the hide of a dogfish is like rough sandpaper which can rub the skin right off an unprotected hand or arm. To avoid this and the possibility of being bitten I always attach my hook traces to a buckle swivel tied directly to the reel line. By doing this it is easy to unclip the trace, drop the huss into a sack, clip on a new trace, and worry about unhooking the catch when I get home. Bull huss have sharp little teeth and a wire hook trace should be used, otherwise many fish will be lost.

I have caught huss during the middle part of a hot sunny day but it is best to fish after dark, for generally speaking bull huss are nocturnal feeders and most of the big fish are caught by the night fishermen. The only practical way of landing a bull huss is to gaff it. The soft white underparts give the best hold for the gaff point. Dogfish make quite good eating although skinning them can be a nuisance. The flesh is rather sweet.

# CHAPTER 9

# Wrasse

Although there are half a dozen varieties of wrasse in our seas, only the ballan wrasse is of interest to anglers, the remainder being small fish which offer little sport on rod and line. The ballan wrasse on the other hand commonly grows to a weight of 5 lb or 6 lb and the rod-caught record ballan wrasse weighed 12 lb 12 oz. This was an exceptional specimen although I am sure that wrasse weighing between 8 lb and 10 lb are more common than is generally supposed. Unfortunately the broad flanks of the ballan wrasse make the fish an ideal target for the spear fishing enthusiast and many outsize ballan wrasse are destroyed in this way each year. Thoughtless anglers also kill a great many prime wrasse, simply because they believe the old story that the wrasse is little more than vermin. It is true that wrasse don't make very good eating and this probably accounts for the attitude of so many sea anglers who make a point of killing every wrasse they catch. Destruction of this kind is pointless and in many areas where wrasse fishing was once good the fish are rapidly beginning to disappear and in time wrasse could locally become a rare species unless anglers learn to take only the fish they require and return all the others they catch alive and unharmed to the sea.

The exceptionally hard winter of 1962–63 further depleted the wrasse stocks, for wrasse are shallow water fish which are extremely susceptible to cold, and because of this many thousands of fine fish perished during that particular winter. Before this period, wrasse fishing was at its best, and there are now signs that wrasse are once again becoming fairly prolific, but thoughtlessness on the part of skin-divers and anglers alike could easily spoil the prospect of future sport with this brightly coloured rock fish. No one really knows just what weight a ballan wrasse can attain, but there is at least one record of a wrasse of over 20 lb in weight, which was said to have floated to the surface after explosives had been used to break up a wreck off the coast of Scotland. A fish of this size would of course be exceptional, and normally any wrasse between 5 lb and 6 lb could be regarded as a good catch. Very few anglers have ever taken wrasse of over 7 lb in weight and my own largest wrasse, which tipped the scales at 9¾ lb, is one of the largest wrasse caught since the war.

Wrasse are essentially rock fish, and a close examination of the external features of a wrasse will quickly show that these fish are well adapted for life among jagged tide-swept rocks. The heavy body scales and thick skin of these fish obviously protect them from serious damage when the currents sweep them into sharp corners of rock. The broad heavy fins of the fish also help it to keep its position when the sea is rough, while the leathery lips and firm teeth of the fish are ideally suited to prising living molluscs off the rocks. Anyone who has caught wrasse will know just how rubbery the lips of these fish are, for once the hook is firmly embedded it is extremely difficult to dislodge.

Ballan wrasse vary considerably in colour from one locality to another, the commonest colour being a greenish-brown. The larger fish are often red and turquoise, or green. Why the larger fish are so brightly coloured no one as yet knows; it could be, however, as the fish grow larger they change their diet which in turn affects their body colour. Some anglers believe that wrasse change their colours to fit in with their surroundings. I personally find this difficult to believe for on many occasions I have taken anything up to twenty wrasse from a single gully, most of which have varied in colour. The larger fish, however, have always been red and turquoise or green. Wrasse are fascinating fish and are well worth a little of anyone's time. Like most species, small wrasse are easily caught and can be a nuisance, but big wrasse are a different proposition and to be consistently successful the keen wrasse angler must be prepared to learn as much as possible about the movement and feeding habits of wrasse.

## Where to Find Wrasse

Wherever the coastline is rocky, wrasse should be found. These fish are most common along our south and south-western shores where the water is fairly warm. I have, however, caught wrasse in the far north of Scotland where the sea is comparatively cold. The coasts of Devon, Cornwall and Wales provide first-class wrasse venues, as do the rocky coasts of Ireland and the Scilly Islands. The Scillies are without doubt the most productive and fish of near record size are known to frequent the rock gullies of these islands. The ideal place to try for wrasse is where a deep weedy gully threads its way between high rocks. Although capable of living in rough water, wrasse show a natural preference for sheltered feeding grounds and a deep gully which is protected from wind and waves provides the shelter which these fish like. The weedier the gully the better the fish like it, for weeds shelter prawns, crabs and other creatures upon which wrasse of all sizes feed. On calm days, wrasse will venture all round the rocks but during periods of rough weather the fish are definitely inclined to seek out the sheltered water.

## Effective Seasons

Although wrasse can be caught throughout the year the most productive months to go wrassing are between April and early October. The warmer the weather, the better the fishing seems to be. July, August and September are the peak periods, and September is the month when one is most likely to catch a monster wrasse.

## Feeding Habits

Small wrasse feed mainly on marine worms, sea loops, and tiny crabs. The medium-sized fish extend this diet to include molluscs, prawns and very small fish. Small crabs are a favourite food of the larger wrasse; small rock fish including tiny wrasse are also taken in large quantities and the angler wishing to catch the largest wrasse will be well advised to employ live crab or fish baits. Live crabs should be hooked through the hind section of the body (fig 94) so that the hook point projects

METHOD OF HOOKING
LIVE HARD BACKED
CRAB

Fig 94

through the shell of the back. Live fish should be lip-hooked (fig 95). Wrasse do not like stale food and in my experience it is rare to catch these fish on bits of mackerel or herring.

LIP HOOKED LIVE BAIT

Fig 95

### Optimum Feeding Times

Wrasse feed best on a rising tide and the most productive period is from half to full tide. During slack water the fish often go temporarily off feed but usually become active again as the tide begins to ebb.

### Bait Collecting

Enough natural bait can be collected at low tide to last for a complete day's fishing. Common limpets can be easily prised off the rocks and although not widely used for other species these shellfish make excellent wrasse bait. Small crabs can also be collected by turning over small boulders. Rock fish of various types also hide in similar places. These should be kept alive in a plastic bucket or livebait holder for they make excellent bait.

## Wrasse Baits (Worms)

Worm baits are the most widely used wrasse baits, and these probably account for more wrasse per season than any other bait. Although worms are undoubtedly good fish catchers I seldom use them, for I have found that the average size of wrasse caught on worm baits is low in comparison to the size caught on other baits. For this reason, I only use worms when other baits are difficult to obtain. Both lugworm and ragworm can be used, and wrasse are not averse to taking broken worm baits. Consequently one large worm can be divided into two or three pieces. Both rag- and lugworm should be threaded on to the hook (fig 96A) for wrasse have strong teeth and will

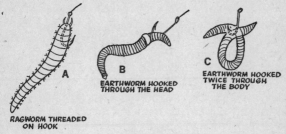

A RAGWORM THREADED ON HOOK

B EARTHWORM HOOKED THROUGH THE HEAD

C EARTHWORM HOOKED TWICE THROUGH THE BODY

Fig 96

quickly clean a hook baited in any other way. A bait which I have successfully used for wrasse, flounders and pollack is the earthworm. I can only presume that a fair quantity of these large landworms find their way into sea water, for wrasse seem to be very fond of them and will take them as well as marine worms. This is useful, for half an hour's digging in the garden or chicken run will usually produce enough worm baits for a

153

good day's fishing. Earthworms are soft when first caught, but they can be toughened up by being stored for a few days in a box full of moss. Worms kept in this way should be examined every day, and any dead or damaged worms should be removed, otherwise all the other worms will die as well. Earthworms should be hooked once through the head (fig 96B) or twice through the body (fig 96C). There is a general belief among sea anglers that earthworms die and turn white when used in salt water. This may be the case when worms are immersed for periods of two or three hours, but for general use, they remain lively and attractive for fairly long periods, and make a good standby bait.

## Fish Baits

Although the brightly coloured cuckoo wrasse which live over rocky offshore grounds feed avidly on fish cutting baits, it is very rare for ballan wrasse to take a bait of this type. These fish will take small livebaits, and I have caught many good wrasse on tiny blennies, gobies and wrasse. Sand eels also make good wrasse bait, but they must be lively, although I once saw a wrasse weighing nearly 10 lb caught on a legered dead sand eel intended for bass. An hour spent turning over stones and groping in shallow rock pools will usually produce a plentiful supply of wrasse-sized livebaits. These can easily be kept in a plastic or metal livebait can, providing, of course, you change the water at frequent intervals and don't overcrowd the baits. Livebaits account for very big wrasse indeed. (See section on livebaiting.)

## Shellfish Baits

I have caught wrasse on a wide variety of shellfish and for all-round wrasse fishing it is hard to find better baits. Common rock limpets are probably the easiest shellfish to gather, for they are prolific in most areas and once the trick of detaching them from the rocks is mastered, they can be collected quickly and easily. The most effective method of dislodging these shellfish is to slip a strong slim knife blade between the relaxed shell of the bait and the rock face. This requires skill and a stealthy approach for the moment it feels a vibration the limpet will clamp itself tightly to the rock. Once this occurs the only way it can be dislodged is to smash the shell with a stone, a wasteful and lengthy process. Once you have learned to use the knife method properly, two or three dozen large limpets can be collected in ten or fifteen minutes.

The large limpets with the orange centres make the best wrasse baits. To keep limpets alive they should be kept in a clean linen bag; carried in this fashion they will remain alive and therefore fresh for a considerable time. When baiting up with limpet the flesh should be extracted from the shell. This is easily and neatly done by inserting and twisting a knife blade between the flesh and shell of the bait. Once the bait has been extracted it is ready for use. I have found that by baiting up so that the point and barb of the hook protrude from the limpet's dark intestine (fig 97), I miss few fish on the strike. Wrasse

DARK INTESTINE

HOOK BAITED WITH LIMPET

Fig 97

often go for this soft section of the bait first and by positioning the hook correctly the fish takes the hook at its first bite. Mussels, scallops and clams also make good bait. At Fowey I have dug big edible clams from the sand in the Fowey River, then cut the flesh into sections and used them as bait for the big wrasse at nearby rock fishing marks.

*Prawn Baits*

There is nothing that a wrasse of any size likes better than a large lively prawn. Fortunately, prawns are often easy to catch in quantity by pushing a small hand net round the weed that grows round submerged rocks. An even better method is the 'drop net' technique. A drop net is sieve-shaped (fig 98) and should be baited with a piece of fish and then lowered on a length of cord or thin rope into deep water where prawns gather in quantity. After the net has been in position for five or ten minutes it should be raised smoothly to the surface. Jerky movements must be avoided for the prawns that are feeding on

FISH BAIT
LASHED TO
CROSSBARS

←LEAD WEIGHT

DROP NET FOR
CATCHING PRAWNS

Fig 98

the fish bait will quickly take alarm and flip over the rim of the net and escape. Drop nets are easy to make and the rim of an old bicycle wheel makes the ideal framework on which to hang the actual netting.

Prawns are sensitive creatures which die quickly if roughly handled or left out of water for any length of time. A tin full of soft wet seaweed is the best thing to carry prawn baits about in. Prawns should be hooked through one of the tail segments so that they remain alive and active in the water. I have found prawns are best when fished on float tackle. In rough water dead prawns are almost as good fish catchers as live prawns, for the action of the waves will make the float bob up and down and impart movement to the bait.

## Crab Baits

Green shore crabs make first-class wrasse bait, and many of the very big wrasse which I have been fortunate enough to catch have fallen to crab baits. Most sea anglers swear by soft or peeler crab bait but for wrasse I find that hard-backed crabs make the best baits. Crabs are easy to gather in quantity and easier still to keep alive so there is seldom any problem in gathering a sufficient supply for a day's wrasse fishing. Crabs the size of a 10p piece make the best bait. These should be used alive. The method I employ to attach them to the hook is as follows. First turn the crab over on its back, then push the hook point through the triangle at the extreme end of the crab's body. The point and barb of the hook should protrude through the back of the crab. A bait mounted in this fashion will remain lively and will be presented to the hunting fish in a natural manner.

## Sea Slaters

A sea slater looks like an overgrown woodlouse and although they are not a favourite bait of mine they make good fish catchers. By nature the sea slater is a nocturnal creature which spends its day hidden away in dark damp rock crevices. They are easily caught after dark for they emerge from their hiding places by the thousand. All that is required to collect them is a torch and a deep tin, the torch being used to pinpoint the slaters as they cling to the rock faces. Once a supply has been collected make absolutely certain that the lid of your bait tin is securely in place, for slaters are adept at escaping and a house full of large slaters is more than most wives or mothers can stand. Sea slaters can be fished on float or paternoster tackle.

## TACKLE

Wrasse have a reputation for being poor fighters, probably because most anglers fish for them with a standard beach-casting outfit. This type of tackle is far too heavy and the angler wishing

157

to specialize in wrasse fishing will be well advised to choose his tackle carefully bearing in mind that the lighter the tackle the better the sport the wrasse will give. At the same time it is essential to use tackle that is capable of stopping a really large wrasse from diving under a rock or other underwater obstruction. This is a favourite and most effective trick which often proves successful. Obviously choosing a light outfit which is still strong enough to control a biggish fish in a rock- and weed-infested gully can present many problems; over the years, however, I have accumulated a set of tackle which I find ideal for all aspects of wrasse fishing.

## Rods

For all-round wrasse fishing a rod should be light enough to hold all day, strong enough to control a largish fish in a confined space, and long enough to apply pressure at any angle. A short rod is useless when it comes to stopping a hooked fish from swimming under a rock ledge almost directly under the angler's feet. A long rod on the other hand will easily turn the fish from its objective. The ideal rod for this sort of work is a 10 ft hollow glass carp rod. This type of rod combines lightness and strength and is more than adequate for any form of wrasse fishing from rocks. A rod of this type will handle lines up to 14 lb comfortably and I have yet to find it necessary to use a line with a heavier bs than this while wrasse fishing.

## Reels

Choice of reels for rock fishing for wrasse is a matter of personal preference and at various times I have used multipliers, centre pins, and fixed-spool reels for this branch of angling. All three have their advantages, but for all-round general use a standard-sized fixed-spool reel is by far the most versatile of the three. Moreover, the slipping clutch mechanism of this type of reel can be invaluable for playing a strong fish in a narrow rock gully. There is little point in using extra-large fixed-spool reels for this form of fishing, for the spool capacity of the standard reel is quite adequate.

## Line

Although wrasse are far from cautious feeders there are times when they show a distinct fear of the line. This usually occurs when a light-coloured line is used. My own experiences lead me to believe that the darker the line colour the less the fish seem to notice it. There are some excellent camouflaged nylon lines on the market: these are ideal. Wrasse live and feed among sunken reefs and barnacle-covered rocks. Consequently the reel line quickly deteriorates and for this reason it is wise to purchase medium-priced lines and to change them fairly frequently during the course of the year.

## Sundry Items

A plentiful supply of $\frac{3}{4}$ oz and 1 oz leads must be carried at all times for when bottom fishing for wrasse a great deal of terminal tackle will be lost on snags. Drilled bullets are ideal, for they are cheaper to buy and equally as efficient as the swivelled bomb-shaped leads which so many anglers use. For float work a supply of $\frac{1}{2}$ oz barrel leads should be carried. A few small barrel swivels are also useful, particularly when float fishing.

## Hooks

Wrasse have large mouths and a size 1 or 2 hook is about the right size for general wrasse fishing. Model perfect, or beaked eyed hooks are best for they are cheap to buy and it doesn't matter if a dozen or more are lost during a day's fishing.

## Float Fishing

In deep flat-bottomed rock gullies, float tackle can be used to good effect. For there will be no obstacles which the terminal tackle can become caught up in. Float tackle can also be used for fishing along the seaward edge of a reef where the bottom is usually composed of sand or shell grit. It pays to use the lightest possible floats for general wrasse fishing, for a large bulky float creates a considerable amount of resistance which can easily cause a biting fish to spit out the bait. There are

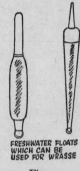

FRESHWATER FLOATS
WHICH CAN BE
USED FOR WRASSE

Fig 99

many good floats available, some of which are primarily designed for use in fresh water (fig 99). Several patterns of small well-designed sea floats are also easy to obtain (fig 100). When choosing a float always bear in mind that its main function is to support the bait at a given depth. The fact that it also serves as a bite indicator is of secondary importance.

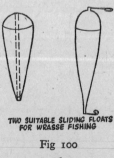

TWO SUITABLE SLIDING FLOATS
FOR WRASSE FISHING

Fig 100

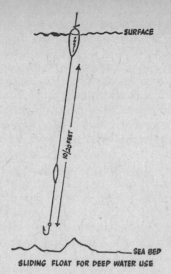

SLIDING FLOAT FOR DEEP WATER USE

Fig 101

For fishing deep gullies a sliding float must be used (fig 101). These rubber stops should be set so that the bait is suspended approximately 6 in above the sea bed. In shallow water a fixed float can be substituted for the sliding type (fig 102). If, however, the intention is to fish a series of gullies during

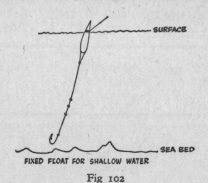

FIXED FLOAT FOR SHALLOW WATER

Fig 102

the course of the day, it is advisable to make the tackle up with sliding float tackle in the first instance so that by moving the rubber stop up and down it is possible to fish any gully irrespective of depth. Live prawns or worm baits are best for float fishing for both are fragile baits which unless fished on delicate tackle are easily nipped off the hook by the biting fish without a clean bite being registered. On light float tackle the slightest mouthings of an interested fish are clearly indicated, and providing the float is watched attentively at all times few bites will pass undetected. When a wrasse of reasonable size takes a prawn or worm bait, the float is usually drawn under without any preliminary warnings. Providing the angler is watching, and the line between rod tip and float is kept taut, very few bites should be missed. Although wrasse are slow to take alarm at unusual movement it is wise to make a point of being as unobtrusive as possible and to wear dark-coloured clothes that blend in with the rocks.

## BOTTOM FISHING

### Legering

In snag- and weed-free water a plain running leger (fig 103) can be used for wrasse fishing. Under any other circumstances, the leger is practically useless, for the action of the tide will quickly roll the weight under a rock or into weed and once this occurs a breakage is almost inevitable. De-shelled limpets are a good leger bait, for they are both attractive to fish and

LEGER FOR USE ON WEED FREE GROUND

Fig 103

tough enough to stay firmly on the hook regardless of tide strength or interference from small fish or shore crabs. If crabs are a nuisance a small section of cork nipped on to the line 2 in or 3 in from the hook will lift the bait up out of reach of these little pests (fig 103).

## The Paternoster

Of all the various types of terminal tackle in general use the paternoster is by far the simplest and most effective tackle to use when wrasse are the quarry. Nothing elaborate is required

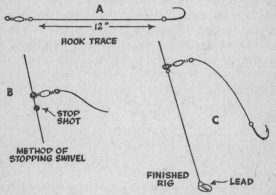

A

← 12" →

HOOK TRACE

B

STOP SHOT

METHOD OF STOPPING SWIVEL

C

FINISHED RIG ← LEAD

THREE STAGES OF MAKING UP A WRASS PATERNOSTER

Fig 104

and the easiest way of making up a wrasse paternoster is as follows. First cut a foot of line from the end of the reel line and tie a small swivel securely to one end (fig 104A). Next pass the end of the reel line through the open swivel eye and stop the swivel with a split shot placed 15 in to 18 in from the end of the reel line (fig 104B). Finally tie a suitable weight to the loose end of reel line, and a hook to the end of the line attached to the swivel, and the tackle is ready for use (fig 104C). Note that only a one-hook paternoster is used, instead of a two- or three-hook rig of the type employed by pier anglers. The reason for using only one hook is simple. Multi-hook tackle is prone to snagging and in a rock gully where snags are abundant a multiple-hook paternoster is more trouble than it is worth. Quite apart from the snagging problems it is quite easy to hook two big wrasse at once on two- or three-hook tackle and if this occurs, the chances are both fish will be lost, for the lightish tackle normally used for wrasse fishing will seldom take the strain of playing two decent fish simultaneously. It is very important to set the tackle so that the baited hook hangs 9 in to 12 in from the sea bed. Hence the fact that the swivel is stopped 15–18 in from the lead. In use the angle of line will suspend the bait at just the right depth if the tackle is set up properly in the first instance. By making certain that the bait is suspended at this depth it is possible to take advantage of the natural groundbait which continuously washes back and forth over the bottom of a rock gully. This groundbait consists of minute particles of edible matter, mixed with dead fish, crabs and molluscs. The wrasse naturally expect to find a great deal of food in this muck and will take a bait presented properly without hesitation. By taking advantage of this it is often possible to catch large bags of big wrasse while other anglers whose baits don't drop among the natural groundbait trail only get the odd fish.

Whole yellow-centred limpets or live crabs make the best baits for this form of wrasse fishing. A wrasse bite on paternoster tackle is normally registered by two or three sharp tugs on the rod tip, followed by a savage pull which whips the rod tip over in a half circle. By waiting until this happens very few true bites will be missed on the strike. Very occasionally a bite will be indicated by the line falling slack. This usually occurs when a biggish fish takes the bait in one gulp and then proceeds to swim towards the rocks on which the angler is standing. Wrasse that do this usually hook themselves. To fish the paternoster properly the line between rod tip and lead weight must be kept taut at all times. This will hold the bait up off the bottom so that it can be clearly seen by the foraging wrasse. By lifting the rod tip and winding in a yard or two of line every few minutes it is possible to thoroughly search every inch of a gully. This is a good idea which will catch far more fish than a static method.

*Livebaiting*

I am inclined to believe that really large wrasse feed mainly on small rock fish and because of this predatory streak I think it unlikely that these extra-large specimens will fall to the more conventional baits which most wrasse anglers use. There must be exceptions to this rule, but many of the largest wrasse ever caught fell to live fish bait of one sort or another, and a number of the outstanding wrasse which I have caught have also been taken on livebait. Almost any small rock fish can be used as wrasse bait, but gobies, blennies and very small wrasse seem to be the best. The only practical method of presenting a livebait is float tackle, which should be set so that the bait is suspended 12 in to 15 in from the sea bed. Big wrasse seem to have no objection to a bait fished in this way, which is fortunate because a livebait fished on or very close to the bottom will soon wedge itself into a crevice or hide among thick weed, where the hunting wrasse will be unable to find it.

Large wrasse have strong teeth and some experienced wrasse anglers make a point of using a wire trace when livebaiting. I am against this because I feel that big wrasse are cautious feeders and will drop a bait mounted on wire. Moreover I have never yet had a wrasse of any size bite through a plain nylon trace, although I have heard various anglers say that they have experienced this problem. There are usually plenty of conger in the wrasse gullies and I am inclined to think that these fish are the culprits responsible for clean-severed traces. One of the handiest floats for wrasse fishing can be made from an empty aluminium cigar tube (fig 105). These can be painted to suit personal requirements and are cheap to make and therefore expendable. This is an important point for the largest wrasse usually inhabit the most snagged-up rock gullies and to be successful the wrasse angler must be prepared to lose quite a lot of end tackle during the course of a day. Shop-bought floats are expensive and very often badly designed. Cigar tubes are easily obtainable, streamlined enough to offer little resistance to a taking fish and yet buoyant enough to support quite a large livebait in a roughish sea.

For livebaiting the trace should be joined to the reel line with a small barrel swivel, otherwise the movement of the livebait will quickly kink and weaken the reel line. A single size 1/0 stainless steel eyed hook is ideal for livebaiting. Treble hooks are unnecessary for wrasse fishing. Livebaiting for wrasse is often a slow sport for the bait is only likely to interest the

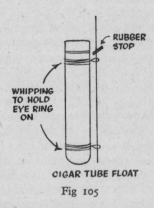

RUBBER
STOP

WHIPPING
TO HOLD
EYE RING
ON

CIGAR TUBE FLOAT

Fig 105

larger specimens which are usually few and far between. For the specialist angler, however, who is only interested in wrasse of specimen size, livebaiting has much to offer and is well worth persevering with. A wrasse bite usually follows a distinct pattern, and the float normally bobs two or three times before sliding under. When using live fish for bait it is essential to give the wrasse time to get the bait well into its mouth. To do this the strike should be delayed far longer than normal, otherwise the bait will be dragged out of the fish's mouth before the hook can penetrate.

## Landing Wrasse

Very often the wrasse angler will be forced to fish from high rocks, which make the landing of big fish extremely difficult. To overcome this problem a landing net with an extendable handle should be used. These can be obtained from any good tackle dealer. Wrasse have little value as table fish and the modern angler normally returns the bulk of his wrasse catches alive and unharmed to the sea. Under no circumstances do I use gaff to land wrasse.

## Handling Wrasse

In some areas the sharp dorsal fin spines of the wrasse are thought to be poisonous. This is nonsense but the tough spines can cut the unwary hand. Because of this it is advisable to handle wrasse of any reasonable size with care. Wrasse should always be returned as gently as possible for they are delicate fish which quickly expire if handled roughly. Big wrasse which have fought strongly are often in an exhausted state when landed and it is often necessary to hold the fish upright in the water until it recovers enough strength to swim off. A wrasse returned in an exhausted condition will simply float on the surface, an easy prey for seagulls. By taking a little trouble with these fish it is possible to ensure sport in future seasons, for it takes a number of years for fish to reach a reasonable size, and unless these big fish are looked after carefully the big fish potential of an area can easily be ruined.

## Playing a Wrasse

The natural instinct of a hooked wrasse is to dive under a rock ledge or other solid obstruction until it feels all danger has passed. To counteract this sudden and powerful plunge the wrasse angler must be prepared to apply maximum pressure as soon as the fish is hooked. If this is done properly the fighting fish will be turned before it can reach its objective and will usually turn and head for open water where it can be easily played right out. If a wrasse does manage to gain the sanctuary it seeks no amount of pulling will shift it, but if the line is slackened so that the pull on the line is relaxed the wrasse will often emerge of its own accord, probably believing that the danger has passed and that it is safe to resume feeding. This line slackening trick has saved a great many fish for me and is well worth remembering. Once they think they are safe, wrasse are bold fish and on more than one occasion when fishing with a friend I have seen wrasse lost and then hooked again still trailing the hook and lead. Very large wrasse are capable of making powerful first runs; fortunately, wrasse tire quickly and once they have burned themselves out during these initial runs they are easy to subdue. Even so, more than one big wrasse has found a new lease of life on sight of the landing net, and until a big fish is safely enmeshed the angler must be prepared for instant action.

# CHAPTER 10

# Flatfish and Other Species

The most common flatfish in British waters is the flounder. These are caught in quantity by the beach and pier fisherman. Harbours and estuaries usually produce the largest specimens.

Flounders vary considerably in colour from one locality to the next, for these handsome little flatfish change colour at will to suit the type of sea bed they happen to feed over. Basically the upper side of the adult fish is dark brown and the underside white, but mottled lighter-backed specimens also occur. I have even seen individual fish which are coloured on both sides. These variations are, however, comparatively rare. Flounders are occasionally confused with dabs. A simple way to identify the fish is to run your hand over its back, for apart from a slight rough patch on the shoulder, the skin of the flounder is smooth and slippery; the skin of the dab, however, is coarse and will feel rough in comparison to that of the true flounder.

Flounders reach a weight of over 5 lb. Most rod-caught specimens, however, average around 16 oz in weight, although fish of over 2 lb are still fairly common.

Flounders are inquisitive little fish that can be caught on a wide variety of baits. Most shore anglers fish for flounders with worm or slipper limpet baits, but fish and squid cuttings, soft-backed crab, earthworms, prawns, mussels and other shellfish can also be used to catch flounders. Flounders can be attracted to a moving bait, particularly one that stirs up the mud and silt as it travels over the sea bed.

Probably the most famous flounder rig is the 'wander tackle' outfit devised by Percy Wadham. As its name implies, the 'wander tackle' works by being kept continually on the move. This rig is particularly useful for beach fishing during calm weather. Wander tackle is easy to make up. First take a 6 ft nylon trace and tie a small barrel swivel to one end. Twelve inches away from this attach a plastic boom with a short nylon trace and size 3 or 4 long-shanked hook. Add a $\frac{1}{4}$ or $\frac{1}{2}$ oz spiral lead six inches below the plastic boom, then between this and the tail hook run a $\frac{1}{4}$ oz ball lead on to the trace and stop it from running down to the hook by pinching a single split shot on to the nylon.

In use, the wander tackle rig is cast out, then wound slowly back over the bottom. The two leads will keep the tackle out straight and also serve to stir up the mud. Flounders usually take a bait boldly and wander tackle often produces two fish at a time.

Many anglers now use a baited spoon for flounder fishing. This rig is ideal for estuary work.

There are many flounder spoons on the market (see fig 106) but I find that the plain white plastic spoons catch more fish than the more ornate heavily chromed metal lures. Flounders will attack a worm-baited spoon on sight; possibly they see the lure as a small flounder dragging a large worm and pounce on the bait in an attempt to drag it away from the smaller fish. Like the wander tackle rig, flounder spoons work best when retrieved slowly across the bottom.

For flounder fishing from open beaches, a plain running leger works well. This rig can be made more attractive by adding one or more red beads to the nylon line directly above the baited hook.

Flounders provide excellent sport on light tackle and to get the best out of these little fish it pays to fish with freshwater spinning style rods, reels and lines.


## Dabs

Dabs can be caught all round our coasts, and almost any sandy bay is likely to hold a stock of these little flatfish. Dabs reach a maximum weight of around 3 lb, but most specimens caught by anglers average 12 to 16 oz in weight.

In colour, the dab is light brown on the back with a faint sprinkling of dark or orange-coloured spots. The underside of the fish is bluish white.

Dabs are caught mainly on worm or mussel baits, but like flounders they will also eat fish and a wide variety of molluscs. Like the flounder, the curiosity of the dab often brings about its downfall. Moving baits attract hunting dabs like a magnet and although these fish seldom fall to flounder spoon rigs, a small shiny button added to the line will often tease them into taking the baited hook.

## Sole

Sole are shy-biting, fast-moving flatfish that can put up a remarkably spirited battle when hooked on fairly light tackle. They reach a weight of over 4 lb, but nowadays any angler who catches a sole of over 2 lb in weight can be proud of his achievement. They are easy to identify, their oval-shaped body and nobbly protruding snout making them a distinctive species. They feed best at night; on beaches where sole are known to live, the best catches are made by anglers who take the trouble to explore the beach at low spring tides, so that they can locate and pinpoint deep gullies. A bait cast into such a gully will usually find sole. Like most flatfish, sole show a liking for fresh water, often congregating at places where a stream or estuary enters the sea.

Worms, razor fish, mussels and shrimps make ideal sole baits, and the tackle can be made more effective still by wrapping a sliver of silver paper round the nylon trace directly above the hook.

During calm weather, particularly at night, sole often move right inshore to feed very close to the beach. Under these conditions, long casting is often a drawback and a bait 'lobbed' twenty to thirty yards will usually produce far more bites than a bait cast out ninety or one hundred yards.

Apart from skate and the very occasional turbot or brill, the heaviest flatfish the shore angler is likely to encounter is the plaice.

Plaice are easy fish to identify, their light backs and vivid orange spots making them impossible to mistake for any other species. Most of the really large plaice caught on rod and line fall to boat anglers, but the shore fisherman can often catch medium-sized specimens in quantity, with the odd outsized fish thrown in to add extra interest to the fishing.

Although plaice are generally caught from sandy beaches and large estuaries, they also occur in harbours and over sandy patches surrounded by rock. I remember catching several very heavy plaice while wrasse fishing with worm-baited leger tackle from the rocks at Hope's Nose near Torquay. Each specimen I caught came from the same area and I decided to investigate the reason for this. Some skin-diving friends supplied the answer for they made an exploratory dive in the area and discovered that there was a largish patch of sand and gravel at this point. Obviously the plaice I was catching were drifting in from the open sea and using this comparatively small area of suitable ground as a base. This gave me much food for thought and made me explore other likely areas in the hope of finding more patches of flatfish ground. In South Cornwall where the sea is usually very clear, it was possible to survey the sea surrounding my usual rock fishing stations. This survey showed many likely spots to try and at various times of the year I made a point of fishing these places with flatfish tackle.

During the autumn, I caught good sole and occasional flounders, while during the early spring and summer the same spots yielded good-sized plaice.

Plaice are comparatively slow-growing fish, but they can reach a weight of 12 or more lb. A 5-pounder caught on rod and line is now regarded as an exceptional specimen, and the average plaice taken by shore fishermen is between 1 and 2 lb in weight. For shore fishing, a plain running leger or a heavier version of the wander tackle rig can be used to catch plaice. Best baits are lugworm, ragworm, slipper limpet and mussel. Sand eels also catch fish, but they must be used fresh. Plaice take a bait gently and to make certain of hooking the fish, it is advisable to give it ample time to take the bait well into its mouth.

## Monkfish and Angler Fish

Both of these fish grow to an immense size and both frequently fall to the shore fisherman. No one fishes deliberately for either species and the specimens that are taken are usually caught accidentally on large fish baits intended for conger. The average weight of both species is between 30 lb and 40 lb, but both fish can exceed 60 lb in weight, although fish of this calibre are rarely landed by rock anglers. Very large specimens of both species are frequently hooked but usually manage to smash the tackle before they can be gaffed or tailed. Many years ago while fishing from the rocks at the eastern end of Polstreath Beach near Pentewan in Cornwall, I surprised an enormous angler fish which was resting in a shallow sheltered gully. I would estimate that this fish weighed well above 60 lb, which made it a possible record-breaker. Naturally I was very keen to catch this particular fish. The trouble was I only had light float tackle with me, and I was fairly certain that my 8 lb line would be too light to control the fish long enough to guide it into shallow water where I would have a chance of beaching it. I tried it, however, and found that getting it to take a chunk of mackerel was no problem nor, for that matter, did it fight much when I set the hook. Its sheer bulk made it impossible to shift and time and again the light line snapped as I tried to induce the great fish to shift from its stationary position on the bed of the gully. Finally at the third or fourth breakage the fish rose to the surface and sailed down the gully and off out to sea.

Since then I have taken several smaller angler fish on heavy bottom tackle and have found that they put up little or no fight. If I had had this type of tackle the day I came across the monster angler at Polstreath Beach I am sure I would now hold the record for this species. Angler fish are ugly, awkward fish, all head and no body. Monkfish are also ugly, but far better proportioned than angler fish, and far more capable of putting up a strong battle when hooked and are more likely to break strong tackle than the angler fish. Both species are far more common in inshore waters than is generally supposed. The angler fish usually turn up on flat sandy ground close to rock, whereas the monkfish, being more active, are likely to turn up almost anywhere. As I have already said, both species are normally only caught accidentally, but I am sure that both could be taken more regularly if fished for seriously. Strong tackle of course would be essential; a wire trace should always be used, for both fish have fearsome teeth which will easily cut through a plain nylon trace. Both fish have huge mouths, so large hooks and big baits can be used with confidence. Bass and conger anglers legering with large squid or fish baits often report being broken up while fishing from rocks. Many of these breakages are probably caused by monkfish or possibly extra-large angler fish. After a prolonged gale is a good time to try for both these species for rough seas tend to drive them inshore in fair numbers, and when one is hooked there will usually be others in the vicinity as well.

*John Dory*

During some seasons large numbers of John Dory appear in West Country waters, where they are often caught by rock and jetty anglers. Dory seldom live in very shallow water but where the rocks fall steeply into deepish open water they can often be observed moving quietly up and down waiting for some small fish to appear. The John Dory is an ugly, awkward fish which exists by preying on small fish of many kinds. They are particularly fond of eating smelt, but small pouting and wrasse are also eaten in large numbers and most of the dory I have caught have been taken on live pouting baits measuring four or five inches in length. John Dory normally swim fairly close to the surface and float tackle is the best type of terminal tackle to use for this species. They have huge mouths and are quick to throw a suspect bait: because of this I prefer to use a treble hook instead of a single hook when livebaiting for them. With a treble the strike can be made the moment the dory sucks in the bait. This usually leads to a well-hooked fish. When a single hook is used many fish will be missed on the strike and a dory which has had a bait dragged out of its jaws can seldom be induced to bite again. Although they normally swim in an upright position they have a novel way of approaching their prey. I have watched these fish hunting and stalking small fish on many occasions and more often than not they turn half over and swim on their sides. In this position they look for all the world like a big harmless flatfish, which is no doubt the way the pout and smelt shoals see them. This gives the predatory dory the chance to get to within striking range and once this happens some luckless little fish is doomed to a sudden death, for dory seldom seem to mistime the final lunge, and presumably the suction power of the big mouth helps to draw the small fish into its jaws. Dory, although ugly, make first-class table fish. The name John Dory is derived from the French *jaune doré* (gilded yellow). Like so many other fish the John Dory is reputed to be the fish that brought the Biblical tribute money: the black spot on its side was supposedly caused by the thumb and forefinger of Saint Peter as he lifted the fish out of the water to take the money from its mouth.

## The Gurnards

Both the grey gurnard and the tub gurnard commonly frequent shallow inshore water and both species are frequently encountered by shore fishermen. Although I have caught both these fish on rocky ground, they are more common where the bottom comprises sand; rock marks surrounded by sand or gravel are ideal places to catch these fish. The best tackle to use is the leger, for gurnard are basically bottom feeders and obtain much of their food from the sea bed. Worm or fish cuttings make the best baits, but gurnard can also be caught on baited spoons (fig 106). This method which was originally devised for catching flounders and other flatfish is a deadly technique where gurnard are concerned. To work properly the spoon should be retrieved very slowly so that it bumps over the sea bed. The clouds of sand and mud which it disturbs greatly attract gurnard. As a general rule gurnard are shoal fish, and

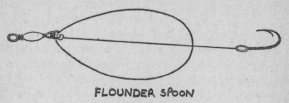

FLOUNDER SPOON

Fig 106

where one is caught there should be others. The average size of shore-caught gurnard is somewhat smaller than those caught by boat anglers, although in Scotland and also Ireland I have caught them up to 3 lb in weight while rock fishing. Along the west coast of Scotland where gurnard are extremely prolific I

PECTORAL 'LEGS'
OF GURNARD

Fig 107

found the best bait was a cutting taken from the side of a salted mackerel. This rather unusual bait caught more fish than a cutting taken from a fresh mackerel. Why this should be I can't say, although gurnard are scavengers and show a liking for offal and rotting fish flesh. Generally gurnard are easy to recognize, for their wedge-shaped heads, and thin tapering bodies make them most distinctive. These fish also possess six leg-like appen-

176

dages with which they walk about over the sea bed. These 'legs' are formed by the last three rays of each pectoral fin (fig 107) which are detached from the rest of the fin rays. Although gurnard do use these rays as a means of locomotion, the true function of these organs is to feel about in the sand or mud for shrimps or other small creatures. Great care should be taken when handling members of the gurnard family for the heads, fins and bodies of these curious fish are very spiky, and although these spikes are not poisonous they can cause deep unpleasant scratches which if left untreated can fester. Despite their odd outward appearance gurnard make good eating, although there is a lot of wastage on each fish. A captured gurnard often emits a series of grunts and groans. These noises are caused by the fish's swim bladders, which are remarkably muscular. Marine biologists say that gurnards grunt to each other under water and the noises are used as signals to other members of the shoal. Despite their strange appearance and awkward shape gurnard put up quite a powerful resistance when hooked on lightish tackle. Along the Welsh coast gurnard are extensively caught by local trawlers. These fish are then dispatched to other parts of the country to be used as bait for lobster pots. When I was a lobster fisherman most of the gurnard I used came from Milford Haven.

## The Rocklings

Although there are several types of rockling, only the three-bearded variety is of any interest to the angler, the other

**HEAD OF THREE BEARDED ROCKLING**

Fig 108

species being too small to be worth bothering with. The three-bearded rockling, which reaches a length of at least 15 in, gets its name from the three barbels which grow from its jaws (fig 108). In colour this rockling is a drab yellowish-brown fish whose body carries a number of dark brown blotches or spots. Rockling are basically nocturnal feeders, which spend most of their life grubbing about amongst the kelp beds in rocky areas. Normally these fish are caught by accident for very few people bother to fish deliberately for rockling despite the fact that on light tackle they put up quite a battle. They fight in fact in an eel-like fashion and many an angler who has hooked a good-sized rocking has convinced himself that he is fast into a small-lish conger. Rockling live on shrimps, molluscs and marine worms. At night they can often be caught in numbers providing the bait is cast out so that it falls among thick rock and weed. A light running leger baited with shrimp or ragworm is more likely to bring results than any other form of terminal tackle.

## The Haddock

Although haddock normally inhabit deep water they can occasionally be caught by shore fishermen particularly along the west coast of Scotland. I have had many medium-sized specimens while fishing from the rocks on the Isle of Arran and also while shore fishing at the mouth of Loch Broom. Haddock as a species have suffered greatly from being over-fished and in many areas where they were once common they are now rarely encountered. This is due to intensive commercial fishing which even now continues to deplete the stocks of these fine fish. The average size of shore-caught haddock is around 16 oz; occasionally a 2 lb to 3 lb fish will be caught but in my experience fish of this size are somewhat rare. Haddock are cod-like fish, but are easy enough to distinguish from the true cod by the pointed first dorsal fin, forked tail, the single dark spot on each shoulder just above the pectoral fin, and the black lateral line (white on cod). The body of the haddock carries no mottlings as does that of the cod. The back of the haddock is purplish-brown in colour and the sides have a silver-bronze sheen. All in all the haddock is a handsome fish, and of all the members of the cod family it makes the best eating. Haddock feed on crabs, shrimps, starfish, and molluscs. They also eat small fish, and most of the haddock I have cleaned have contained various types of fish: sprats, small herring and dragonets seem to be most commonly eaten. Most of the haddock I have caught have been taken on one- or two-hook paternoster tackle baited with fish cuttings, worms or cut-up clam baits. I have also had a few fish on whole mussels. In Scottish waters haddock provide good sport to the shore angler, for they are bold biters and can usually be caught in large numbers.

## The Pouting

Pouting are despised by the majority of sea fishermen, for they are prolific in most areas and make a considerable nuisance of themselves by taking or worrying baits intended for more worthwhile species. The only time pout are truly welcomed is during sea fishing competitions where they help to make up weight in individual catches. Apart from this saving grace they are generally regarded as useless. Pouting are always hungry and ever on the lookout for food. Moreover they move about in vast shoals and on multi-hook tackle can be caught at the rate of two or three to each cast. Almost anything can be used as bait to catch pouting, for they are by no means fussy feeders. Nothing special is required in the way of terminal tackle either, and paternoster or leger are both suitable. Pouting seldom fall to float tackle for they normally feed right on the sea bed.

In appearance the pouting is a chubby, brassy little fish, with a large eye and prominent chin barbel. In colour the pouting is coppery on the back and bronze on the sides. The underparts are pale. Pouting caught over rocky ground often have dark vertical bars on their sides. These tend to fade soon after the fish is dead. Pouting have been known to reach a weight of 4 lb to 5 lb. Most shore-caught specimens weigh less than a pound, and many weigh only a few ounces. Even small pouting have big mouths and sharp little teeth, and they think nothing of attempting to swallow baits almost as

179

large as themselves. Sea fishing novices usually waste a great deal of time and bait in catching multitudes of tiny pouting for which they have no use. In this respect the pouting performs a useful function for it will bite at almost any time of the day, and being easy to catch it encourages newcomers to sea fishing to take up the sport seriously. The only other thing that can be said in favour of the bait-robbing pouting is that it makes wonderful live- or deadbait for bass, conger, skate, ling, etc. Pouting must be used soon after they are caught for once dead they quickly decompose, which is why many commercial fishermen refer to pouting by the nickname 'stink alive'.

## Sea Bream

It is rare for shore anglers to catch black bream, for these handsome sporting fish seldom venture to within casting range of the shore although I once caught a few of these fine fish while casting from the flat rocks at Chapman's Pool, Dorset.

Red bream, on the other hand, are frequently caught by shore fishermen along the south coast of Cornwall and although they don't reach any great size in inshore waters they provide excellent sport for the light tackle enthusiast. The red bream is easy to identify. It is a high-shouldered, short-nosed fish, with a long, sharp dorsal fin. The eyes are large and the pectoral fins are long and sickle shaped. Large specimens are red on the back with lighter sides, and with silvery-pink underparts. There is also a conspicuous black patch on the shoulders.

The smaller fish that the shore fishermen catch are more silvery pink, and often lack the dark shoulder spot. These fish are usually called 'chads'. By nature chad are nocturnal feeders which generally start to take baits as the light begins to fade. They are omnivorous feeders and practically any bait can be used to take them. In my experience they are best caught on fish cuttings for this type of bait stays on the hook well and can be used over and over again. Worm baits which are expensive to buy and difficult to dig are too good to waste on fish like the red bream and should be saved for more fussy feeders. In Cornwall float fishing is the method most used to catch red bream from the shore. This is an excellent and most productive technique which will catch large numbers of these obliging fish – but if quality rather than quantity is required my advice would be to use a light single-hook paternoster, for the larger fish seem to congregate close to the sea bed. Red bream make fair eating, but most of those caught from the shore are a little on the small side to warrant extensive preparation. Chad also make good conger bait.

*Thornback Ray*

There are many types of skates and rays in our seas, but only one is likely to fall fairly often to the shore angler. This is the thornback ray, or roker. Normally these fish frequent areas of sand, mud or gravel. This sort of ground is often found within casting range of shore fishing stations, and with modern tackle and new casting techniques many sea anglers now find themselves capable of casting their bait out far enough to reach likely thornback ground. The average weight of shore-caught thornback is between 6 and 10 lb and as these fish make good eating, they make an ideal quarry for the angler who likes to catch largish fish which provide him not only with good sport but with excellent food as well. In colour the thornback ray is brown on the back, and has a number of pale and dark blotches covering this basic hue. The underside is white and the back and tail are studded with patches of small hooked spines. The tail is usually armed with the largest spines.

Thornback rays eat various types of crabs, small fish, prawns, sand eels, molluscs, and worms. A bunch of big lugworms makes a first-class thornback bait, but peeler and soft crab, and fish baits are all good lures. A live pout or fresh dead pouting is one of my favourite baits, but I have had plenty of good rays on the other baits listed. When fishing for thornback rays I like to use a wire trace because the strong rough lips of the rays can crush or distort even heavy nylon to such an extent that it snaps under strain. For worm baits a size 2/0 hook should be used and for larger baits a 4/0 or 5/0 is ideal. The only practical terminal tackle to use for catching these rays is a running leger. Fairly substantial tackle should always be employed for although thornback cannot be classed as true fighting fish their sheer bulk and habit of kiting away against the tackle makes them difficult to land. When thornback are expected a gaff should be carried. This is the only instrument that can be used to land these fish with any degree of certainty.

# CHAPTER 11

# Local Names for Shore Fish

Many years ago when I first started sea fishing, I was often confused by the local names of the fish I caught. At the same time I started to keep notes of these names and now I have a substantial list of local fish names which I find most useful. Many anglers write or speak to me on this subject and it would seem that they have found it difficult to identify some of the fish they have caught simply because other anglers have called the fish by an unfamiliar name. This sort of thing occurs mainly when anglers spend their holidays fishing a new area which produces fish they have seldom if ever seen before. To try to overcome this problem I give a list of local names for the various fish mentioned in this book.

## Bass

Salmon bass, sea perch, sea wolf, white mullet, sea dace, king mullet, gaple, sand bass, white salmon and gapemouth. Immature bass are often called 'schoolies'.

## Cod

The only local name used by anglers is codling. This is used when speaking of cod weighing under 6 lb. Commercial fishermen use the names rock cod, tamlin, tamblin, and sprags to differentiate between fish of various sizes.

## Haddock

Trawlermen call haddock by the name 'ducks'.

## Conger

Small conger are sometimes called whips or straps.

## Garfish

Sea pike, longnose, sea needle, horn eel, greenbone, Spanish mackerel, mackerel guide and erle.

## Mackerel

'Joey', a name applied to small fish only.

## Mullet

No local names that I can trace.

## Pollack

Whiting pollack, whiting cole, skeet, leet, lythe, greenling, and quay nag.

## Coalfish

Greywond, saithe, black jack, black pollack, rawning pollack, glassaw, green cod, saidhean, cuddle, cudden, blue black, billet, sillock, slyeen, coalman, herring hake, blockan, bleck, coalsey, coal whiting, colmey, billiard, green whiting, gull fish, keeler, lob, sethe, piltock, dargie, harbyne, sey pollack, glassock, and stewlock.

## Tope

White hound, ciglas, penny dog, toper, stink hound, miller dog, blue dog, and sweet william.

# SHARKS

*Porbeagle*

No local names that I can find.


*Thresher*

Sea fox, fox shark, sea ape.

## DOGFISH

*Greater Spotted Dogfish*

Bull huss, nurse hound, bounce.


*Lesser Spotted Dogfish*

Sandy dog, rough hound, row hound, blind jimmy, curfish, kennet, dagger, hund fish, suss, land dog and morgay.

## WRASSE FAMILY

*Ballan Wrasse*

Old ewe, sea swine, sweet lips, old wife, Donovan's wrasse, merrin and spotted wrasse.


*Corkwing Wrasse*

Cowner, corkling, gilt head.

# Index

*James Herriot*

IT SHOULDN'T HAPPEN
TO A VET                                        30p

The text of this book is included in the
American bestseller
*All Creatures Great and Small*

'The happiest book of the year' — NEW YORK
TIMES

Straight from the horse's mouth ...

The things that shouldn't happen to a vet
happened to James Herriot amidst some mem-
orable characters, both animal and human,
in the beautiful Yorkshire Dales.

'His easy and at times excruciatingly funny
case history narratives must rate as country
classics and he throws in a stumbling, awkward
courtship for good measure' — FARMERS'
WEEKLY

'A warm prize of a book' — TIME MAGAZINE

*James Herriot*

IF ONLY THEY COULD TALK    30p

The text of this book is included in the
American bestseller
*All Creatures Great and Small*

'The happiest book of the year' – NEW YORK
TIMES

How now, brown cow . . .
The genial misadventures of James Herriot, a
young vet in the lovely Yorkshire Dales, are
enough to make a cat laugh – let alone the
animals, if only they could talk.

'One of the best countryside books I have read
in years . . . full of life and fun with an
imaginative touch which makes the most of
the fine scenery and rich characters of the
Dales' – OXFORD MAIL

'Lively, vivid and very funny' – SUNDAY
EXPRESS